What people are saying about …

enough

"Can a book be hard-hitting without being guilt-inducing? Can it be both convicting and encouraging? Can it be beautifully written and deeply thoughtful—and really funny in places too? Can it be good for you and enjoyable to read? Can it help intensify your commitment to God and decrease your addiction to stuff? With Will Samson's *Enough*, the answers are all yes."

Brian McLaren, author and activist, brianmclaren.net

"The problem is not us owning things; the problem lies in things owning us. Will Samson reminds us not to confuse Christianity with Capitalism. *Enough* is a hopeful invitation to begin banking in God's economy and reimagine what it means for followers of Jesus to prosper. Enthusiastically recommended."

Matthew Sleeth, MD, director of
www.blessed-earth.org and author
of *Serve God, Save the Planet*

"Will Samson calls the Christian family to the table for a veritable feast of information and inspiration on how to live in peace, community, and simplicity. *Enough* is not to be missed."

Claudia Mair Burney, author of *Zora
and Nicky* and *Wounded*

"Will Samson has caught a glimpse of the abundance that promises more than your best life now. Inspired by the Eucharist, Will outlines a life better than we could imagine in our cultural captivity—an economy of enough where the poor find bread and the rich find contentment because we find one another in the community of our Lord. Read the book but more than that, join the feast.

Jonathan Wilson-Hartgrove, new monastic, author, and director of School for Conversion

enough

enough

Contentment in an Age of Excess

WILL SAMSON

David C Cook®

transforming lives together

ENOUGH
Published by David C. Cook
4050 Lee Vance View
Colorado Springs, CO 80918 U.S.A.

David C. Cook Distribution Canada
55 Woodslee Avenue, Paris, Ontario, Canada N3L 3E5

David C. Cook U.K., Kingsway Communications
Eastbourne, East Sussex BN23 6NT, England

David C. Cook and the graphic circle C logo
are registered trademarks of Cook Communications Ministries.

The Web site addresses recommended throughout this book are offered as a
resource to you. These Web sites are not intended in any way to be or imply an
endorsement on the part of David C. Cook, nor do we vouch for their content.

All Scripture quotations, unless otherwise noted, are taken from the *Holy Bible, New
International Version*®. *NIV*®. Copyright © 1973, 1978, 1984 by International Bible
Society. Used by permission of Zondervan. All rights reserved. Scripture quotations
marked ESV are taken from *The Holy Bible, English Standard Version*. Copyright © 2000;
2001 by Crossway Bibles, a division of Good News Publishers. Used by permission.
All rights reserved. NRSV are taken from the New Revised Standard Version Bible,
copyright 1989, Division of Christian Education of the National Council of the
Churches of Christ in the United States of America. Used by permission. All rights
reserved. KJV taken from the King James Version of the Bible. (Public Domain.) MSG
taken from THE MESSAGE. Copyright © by Eugene H. Peterson 1993, 1994, 1995,
1996, 2000, 2001, 2002. Used by permission of NavPress Publishing Group.

Italics in Scripture are added by the author for emphasis.

LCCN 2008911399
ISBN 978-0-7814-4542-9

© 2009 Will Samson
The author is represented by MacGregor Literary

The Team: Andrea Christian, Amy Kiechlin, Sarah Schultz, and Jaci Schneider
Cover Design: Big [Brand Innovation Group, LLC] Creative Team
Cover Photos: istockphoto

Printed in the United States of America
First Edition 2009

2 3 4 5 6 7 8 9 10

050109

This book is dedicated to Communality,
a community of people who continually remind me what it means
to be taken, blessed, broken, and given to the world.

Contents

How to Read This Book   11

Foreword   13

Introduction   17

Chapter 1 - People Consumed by Stuff **29**

The Story of Stuff   33

Why All This Stuff?   34

All Kinds of "Stuff"   36

Chapter 2 - Communities Consumed by God **41**

Moral, Therapeutic Deism   42

Civil Religion   44

Wait, Weren't We Talking About Consumerism?   48

Chapter 3 - My God Is So Big **53**

The Death of [God]   56

God in the Gutenberg Galaxy   58

Calling All Prophets   60

God, Speaking to the American Church: 61

Chapter 4 - Flannelgraph Jesus **65**

Jesus and "the Other"   68

Jesus and Sustainability   71

Jesus and Life   73

Chapter 5 - I Wish We'd All Been Ready **77**

The Spirit of the Antichrist   80

Samson's Wager   83

Reimagining Readiness   84

Chapter 6 - The Eucharist and the Social Construction of Theology **87**

Defining The Eucharist   90

Eucharistic Communities   92

Communities Of Moral Formation   95

Chapter 7 – Body **99**

Lifestyle Diseases 99

The Mind-Body Connection 103

Pornographication 105

Some Suggestions 107

Chapter 8 – Earth **111**

Food 113

Energy 116

Just The Beginning 117

Some Suggestions 118

Chapter 9 – Economy **123**

God is Not a Capitalist 126

Paying for the Party 131

Some Suggestions 133

Chapter 10 – Community **137**

Fragmented Lives 138

Fragmented Communities 142

The Loss of a Moral Center 144

Some Suggestions 144

Chapter 11 – The Practices of

Eucharistic Communities **149**

Practice God's Presence 150

Practice the Belief in Enough 151

Practice Gratitude 152

Practice Celebration 154

Practice Giving 154

Chapter 12 – To Be **157**

To Be Converted 158

To Be Whole 159

To Be Consumed 160

A Closing Prayer 161

References and Notes 163

How to Read This Book

This is a book about consumerism, contentment, and following Jesus. Other books have been written about consumerism and contentment that don't take into account what it means to be a follower of Jesus, and you should read those also. But this is not that book. This is a book by a follower of Jesus, for followers of Jesus.

Don't skip the introduction. If you are like me, you are tempted to jump around in a book. You can do that with the other sections. But don't skip the intro.

The first section of this book (chapters 1–6) is more thoughtful and less practical. If you are fairly well convinced you know what Jesus, Scripture, and the tradition of the church have to say about the issue of consumption, you can skip to section two (chapters 7–10), which has lots of numbers and data, and includes some practical steps for moving beyond mindless use of stuff.

But make sure you read the third section. In that I attempt to cast a vision for what our communities of faith can look like if we are willing to move in rhythm with God's heartbeat for the world. And, I try to leave you with some encouraging words.

I trust that you enjoy this book. Feel free to e-mail me, and I will get back to you as best as I can: will@willsamson.com.

Foreword
by Shane Claiborne
activist and author of *The Irresistible Revolution*

This book is not a self-righteous rant. We don't need any more of those.

This book is not a guilt-trip. Guilt can be a good indicator of where things are wrong, but it's a bad motivator toward things getting right.

This book is not a trendy how-to book on ecofriendly living. Those may actually be pretty sweet … that's just not what this is.

This book is an invitation to reimagine the way we live.

I am writing this foreword in the frenzy of the holidays, with Black Friday, the biggest shopping day of the year, just a few hours behind us. It is a strange thing that we celebrate the birth of the homeless, refugee, born-in-a-genocide Jesus by buying stuff—nearly $450 billion worth of stuff. This year was terrible. News stories told of fights, riots, and stampedes that happened all over the country. One news story even told of a thirty-four-year-old Wal-Mart worker who was trampled to death underneath the feet of a salivating mob in a feverish rush to save a few bucks on a plasma TV. Eventually we stand back in horror, pity, or embarrassment and ask—how did we get to this point?

Enough.

One of the things we do every year in our community on Black Friday is go to the mall and throw a "Buy Nothing Day" party with all sorts of fun circus whatnots, free stuff like hot cocoa and hugs, and alternative ideas for taking the holiday season back as a time for compassion not consumption. One of my favorite memories is of a woman who came up to me with an ear-to-ear grin and said, "Thank you. I just needed permission to say ENOUGH!—ENOUGH to the frenzied rush to buy stuff for people who already have everything."

In these pages, Will Samson gives you permission to say "Enough!" Sometimes we just need an excuse.

"Enough" to the myth that happiness must be purchased. "Enough" to an economy that is awarding CEOs salaries five hundred times that of their workers and still manages to seduce people in poverty and wealth alike to give more money to these predatorial corporations. "Enough" to the advice of government leaders who fearfully order us to "just keep shopping" after tragedies like September 11. "Enough" to the American dream that now consumes over 40 percent of the world's stuff with less than 6 percent of the world's resources. "Enough" to a dream that would need four more planets if the world pursued it … a dream the world cannot afford. ENOUGH.

Maybe God has another dream.

Will invites you to enter the story of a God who is forming a people who are peculiar to the patterns of nations and empires and markets. We see there a God who sets in place peculiar practices like Jubilee and gleaning to insure that the poor are cared for and inequality is dismantled. We see a God who warns the people that if they do not say "Enough" to the patterns of empire, then those patterns will destroy them.

And we see prophets like Ezekiel that decry the sins of civilizations like Sodom (from where we get the word sodomy) saying: "Now this was the sin of your sister Sodom: She and her daughters were arrogant, overfed, and unconcerned; they did not care for the poor and the needy" (Ezek. 16:49). Arrogant. Overfed. Unconcerned.

Will is a prophet of the 'burbs, a gentle voice in the wilderness of suburbia who begins with the log in his own eye rather than trying to dig the speck out of yours. He rips open the pages of Scripture with the hope that another world is possible, that indeed God does have another dream from the world than Wall Street.

There could not be a better time for this book. Headlines across the land in this experiment called America show us how fragile our world and economy have become. I have a newspaper I've kept that has two front-page articles exemplifying the crisis. One cover story was about a village in Afghanistan where children have become so desperate that they are eating grass to stay alive. The other feature article told of obesity in America and how we are eating ourselves to death, and how over 300,000 deaths annually could be prevented if people simply did not overconsume. Our world is sick.

We live in a world trapped in the ghettoes of poverty and the ghettoes of wealth. Here in the United States, we are some of the richest folks in the world ... but also some of the most lonely, depressed, and medicated. This book is a call to life to the fullest, a way of living that liberates those stuck in poverty and those stuck in the cul-de-sacs. But this book is good news. It is not simply a NO to the things wrong in the world. Will invites us to say YES to another way of doing life.

There is a promise in Scripture that there is enough, that God did not mess up and make too many people or too little stuff. There is enough. One of the first stories is of how God rained down bread from heaven (Ex. 16). And the miracle is followed with a commandment:

"Take only your daily bread and there will be enough for everyone."
And there was enough. Throughout the biblical narrative, there is
the promise of providence, that God will provide this day our daily
bread. In the New Testament, Paul scolds the church at Corinth for
taking more than they needed while others had less, saying: "At the
present time your plenty will supply what they need so that in turn
their plenty will supply what you need. Then there will be equality,
as it is written: 'The one who gathered much did not have too much,
and the one who gathered little did not have too little'" (2 Cor.
8:14–15). There will be ENOUGH. As Gandhi said so well, "There
is enough for everyone's need but there is not enough for everyone's
greed." Paul goes on to scold the young Christian movement in their
practice of the communion feast because some people are coming to
the Lord's table hungry while and others are overstuffed or drunk (1
Cor. 11:20). They have desecrated the vision of the Eucharist.

Will Samson calls us to be a people of the Eucharist, a people
who do not take more than this day their daily bread and do not
store up in barns stuff for tomorrow. Will invites us to experience
the freedom the lilies and the sparrows who do not worry about
what to eat or what to wear or about a 401(k) plan, but those lilies
and sparrows live in the simplicity of God's loving provision and in
their simplicity they shame Solomon and Beverly Hills in all their
splendor. Will rejects the nihilistic myth of scarcity and sets straight
the self-centered, blessing-obsessed gospel of prosperity.

Here is a beautiful invitation to live simply that others may
simply live.

Introduction

It has been another one of those weeks. You know, a week where you wish you could sell everything and go somewhere, anywhere, and do anything but what you are doing now. Work is disappointing again, and you wish you had the time and the money to change careers, go back to school, or start that business you've dreamed about for years. But there are children in your house who need clothes and food, and your spouse depends on you too.

You want to "thank God it's Sunday," but it's all you can do to drag yourself out of bed, shower, help with the toast and jam, pile everyone into the car, and turn your vehicle onto the road in the direction of church. *Maybe this Sunday will be different,* you tell yourself. Maybe God will come near, maybe you will sense a touch of the divine, maybe you will leave the building with something more than some scribbled notes that you'll eventually forget and discard.

You desperately want God to come near in a very real way. You want the service to give you something to take home, something to transform your day-to-day, humdrum life, something that will give you meaning. You've been hoping for that sort of experience for several years now. Every once in a while it happens and, at least for a few days afterward, you feel a sense of renewal, a sense of hope in the process of becoming holy, hope in the process of becoming more whole. You long for that wholeness.

After taking the kids to their classes, you slide into the pew of the sanctuary to listen to the adult education class. This week is something about spiritual gifts and how you can serve in the church. *Hmmm, there's a new one*, you comment sarcastically to yourself.

As your eyes wander around the sanctuary, a sense of relief glides over you when you view the table before the pulpit with the words "Do This in Remembrance of Me" carved in Old English letters on its front. Atop the table, brass trays glimmer in the light of the overhead chandelier.

It's Communion Sunday. Thanks be to God. You only need to wait an hour until the sacrament is given. Not much longer.

Jesus has always been real to you in Communion. You're not sure why. There is definitely a sense of obligation to this ceremony—Jesus asked his disciples to carry on the tradition, and it is one of the few things the church has always done. But your connection to this ceremony is deeper. Something holy happens during Communion: the silence; the soft piano playing; even the fact of this whole group of people, eating the little chunk of bread and drinking juice from the plastic cup. It may be the only time all these people are in agreement on anything.

But this is also truly a time of remembrance. As you eat the bread and drink the cup, you will remember Christ's sacrifice, his love, his life, his grace, and his never-ending mercy. You need that memory. You need this act.

Soon enough, the kids join you for the service. The crowded sanctuary is mostly a mix of familiar faces, although looking from the back row of the church, you are mostly viewing familiar heads: the lady with the big hat, the teenagers who are never found apart, and the young mom who comes to church alone.

After some hymns, the offertory, Scripture, and special music, the pastor delivers his sermon. *Wasn't that the sermon he used the last time he preached through Romans?* Oh well, no problem. He's a charismatic preacher, and it never hurts to be reminded. Throughout the sermon you again look at the Communion table assembled up front. The gold plates filled with bread and little cups of juice, the white linens that are laundered and ironed by one of the older women in the church.

Soon you will "take Communion." It seems such an odd phrase—to "take Communion." But it's a ritual you know well. You've been doing it almost all of your life. A few years ago, you took it for granted, but now that you're maturing a bit, you've been finding it more and more meaningful.

Finally, the sacrament begins. A loaf of bread is broken as Christ's body was broken. Juice is poured out, telling the story of sacrifice and atonement. Plates are passed with these elements to share in the Eucharist. A sense of excitement runs through you as you wait for Communion to come to you and your family.

But as the plates are being passed, you begin to notice some strange activities. The woman in the big hat grabs a handful of bread cubes and shoves them in her mouth, then she takes another handful and stuffs them in her purse. Her children are following the mom's lead, cramming bread into pockets as the usher tries to wrangle the plate away from them. You elbow your spouse who, mouth dropping, can't believe it either.

And now, the teenagers seem to have some kind of a party with the little cups of juice, downing them like shots, clinking the small glasses together and laughing loudly. Oh sure, they look like they're having the time of their lives, but this isn't what this meal is for.

Surely Jesus didn't die just so some people could grab it all, while others are left out.

What is happening here? You want to stand up and scream, "Stop!" But the plates keep getting passed, others following suit with the party crowd, and by the time the elements reach you, there is nothing left. No bread. No cup. Nothing.

There was supposed to be enough. Wasn't there?

How do we think about this question of *enough*? The Eucharist is a good place for a Christian to start, simply because, for nearly two thousand years, since the inception of Christianity, there has never been a day when some Christians somewhere in the world did not gather together to break bread and drink from the cup to celebrate the work of Christ. It is the most common experience of the church throughout its life, and an important metaphor to explore as we work through these pages.

Thinking about the common table of Christianity will help us get beyond some of the simple economic questions often asked in conversations about consumerism and resources. Not that we shouldn't think economically, mind you; but we need a richer, deeper exploration of this issue than basic calculations of "more and less" can provide.

We will explore some other metaphors together as well. The idea of the body has a lot to contribute to the questions we will ask. Christ's body was broken so that we might be whole. The church is spoken of as the body of Christ. Paul employs the body as a metaphor to speak of the sufficient enabling of the church to completely participate in God's work in the world.

The metaphor of the Trinity will come up in our conversation on these pages. Since the earliest days of the church we have struggled to understand a God who is one, yet three. A man who was God, without origin, and yet could say, "As the *Father* has loved me, so I have loved you. Now remain in my love" (John 15:9). And the church has continually struggled to understand the implications for our communities: If God exists in a social relationship, what does that say about our existence? If we are made in the image of this social God and are meant to create communities that reflect that union, how does that affect the way we think about our resources? Is there an understanding of our use of resources that is consistent with our understanding of God?

We will talk about other metaphors used throughout Scripture and the tradition of the church. We will also speak of the importance of story and narrative, and of the idea of lives lived as gifts given on behalf of a world in need.

But before we can get to the rich ideas that might help us imagine a new way of living in the world, I need to tell you about my motivation for writing this book. To understand the whole of my story I want to give you a bit of a look back. About four years ago I had realized the American dream, or at least was fast on my way toward it. I had two Volvos, three kids, and a five-thousand-square-foot house. Everything was coming up sevens. But, like a consistent majority of Americans, I did not feel content with the dream.

I was raised in conservative theological circles and raised to be a world changer. Four years ago, my life just didn't feel very revolutionary.

All around me people struggled to make ends meet. Their ends were not the elementary struggles of life: None of my neighbors wondered where their next meal was coming from, but some wondered if they would have enough money after meeting the mortgage payments to actually buy furniture for their house. How crazy is that?

All around me people seemed caught in a bizarre race against each other, time, expectations of culture, and their own sense of what their lives were meant to be about. Most, I would guess, had more material wealth than their grandparents could have imagined possible. Yet for the majority it was not enough. It seemed they would never be satisfied.

Part of my life journey the past few years has been to ask what it means to live with enough; to live in rhythm with God's economy; to truly live. I will explore some of that as we go along. But four years ago, when I started asking some of these questions in earnest, I was working as a successful business consultant in Washington, D.C. After a nasty experience in the dot-com world of the late nineties (yes, I was one of those people) and some personal losses, such as the death of my mother-in-law, we had recovered quite nicely. My wife, Lisa, and I had a lovely home in suburban Baltimore. We had the money to travel where we wanted, eat what we liked, and wear what was fashionable, within reason.

But our lives were not just a senseless string of consumer choices. We were deeply engaged with the church. I was working bivocationally as the director of Christian ministries for a church plant where Lisa served as the worship leader. Our kids attended youth group. We participated in "friendship evangelism" days when we served the community in real and tangible ways.

We were living the model American Christian life. We had nice kids, great jobs, fun cars, and still found time and a bit of money for the church. Why wasn't I happy?

To understand the answer to that question, we have to go back a few more years. I was raised in a Bible church, which is kind of like being a Baptist, only in New Jersey. My view of culture was very conservative. I remember a four-week sermon series from the pastor in the church where I was raised about the evils of substitute blasphemy. After that we weren't allowed to say "gee" or "gosh" in my house for a really long time.

But the church was also truly a *Bible* church, which meant that my view of Scripture was very conservative as well. From an early age I learned the word *inspiration*, like in the famous verses from Paul's second letter to Timothy: "All scripture is given by inspiration of God, and is profitable for doctrine, for reproof, for correction, for instruction in righteousness: That the man of God may be perfect, thoroughly furnished unto all good works" (2 Tim. 3:16–17 KJV). The inspiration of the Bible meant that it came from the very breath of God (other translations of the verses above use the phrase *God-breathed*). Scripture, then, was from the very mouth of God. Not to be debated, simply to be followed.

Even as a child, however, I often wondered why it seemed we followed some parts of Scripture, but not others. Why, for example, were the Ten Commandments such a rule for life, but not the Sermon on the Mount? If all of Scripture was inspired, why did I almost never hear sermons based on the Minor Prophets?

The inspiration of the Bible was also closely linked to another concept: *infallibility*. In other words, the Bible did not contain errors. The sum of these two beliefs was that my view of the Bible while I was growing up was quite high. It trumped all other questions.

This is still the understanding of the Bible in much of the American Protestant Christian church. In fact, I remember one time during my years in lay ministry, after I had begun to come into a broader understanding of Scripture, that I suggested the following line in a church where I was ministering to describe the view of the Bible: "The Bible is the story of God's faithfulness to his people throughout generations." But that description wasn't allowed. Can you guess why? That's right: The Bible is not a *story*.

Politically, I was raised to be conservative as well. Like Alex P. Keaton, the stereotypically conservative character on the NBC show *Family Ties* who supported Ronald Reagan, I took the pro-Nixon side in my third-grade class debate. The scandals of that administration were one of the few cultural events I have ever seen cause my father to be visibly upset.

In the world of my youth, cultural, biblical, and political orthodoxy were all the same. To accept the authority of the Bible in one's life meant to vote Republican and not to smoke, drink, chew, or go with the girls who do.

As a student at Jerry Falwell's Liberty University in the 1980s, I read the works of Russell Kirk and Ludwig von Mises and subscribed to *National Review*. William F. Buckley became my hero. I bought a tweed blazer. As a Christian conservative, I voraciously consumed the writings of Francis Schaeffer, especially his later works that called for the radical political engagement by the church in hot-button issues like abortion.

I was deeply engaged in politics during the 1980s and early 1990s, driven largely by my involvement in the pro-life movement. I worked professionally as a campaign organizer for mostly state and local Republican candidates, most of whom were pro-life, but all of whom were probusiness. During those years I struggled alongside a recognizable cast of characters, including the Christian Coalition, The Traditional Values Coalition, the Leadership Institute, National Right to Life, Concerned Women for America, the NRA, and the Home Builders.

I left politics in 1994 after the Republicans' Contract with America brought about a complete takeover of Congress. As naïve as it sounds now, I believed *we* had *won*. At the time, my understanding of who "we" were and what it would mean for us to "win" was somewhat limited, but I nonetheless bowed out of politics after eight years, expecting morality to reign throughout our nation.

That didn't work out so well.

In fact, in the years since then I have experienced a bit of shift in my understanding of Scripture, politics, and culture. I will talk about that throughout the book as it relates to our conversation. But, I wanted to give you a bit of my story, because it is deeply ingrained in who I am and how I view the world.

And where I came from also serves to explain my discontentment with the state of the church and my journey to live into a richer understanding of God's economy. This book is a reflection of one part of that journey, a journey to move more fully into a view of the world that is seen with God's eyes.

It is also an attempt for me to work out some of the thoughts I have been having lately. Here is an overview of those thoughts, which also provide a kind of summary-level understanding of this book:

1. As a culture and as a church, we have become consumed with the idea of stuff. Our value as persons, even as Christians, is often judged by how much stuff we have. When we are short on stuff, we sometimes think God is mad with us. When we have a lot of stuff, we remember to thank God, but usually only briefly, before we consume our stuff.

2. We are not consumed by an incarnational God the same way we are consumed by stuff. We also probably do not believe that God is sufficient.

3. As Christians, we are not without resources to answer questions about what is enough.

4. The best resource we have for walking in step with God's heartbeat for the world is the life and model of Jesus.

5. To address questions of what is enough and how we live, part of what needs to be rethought is how we think about the future and how that should shape our actions. If we truly believe the world is going to end tomorrow, why are we still building large churches? Or, if we are still building churches and homes and universities, do we truly believe the world is going to end tomorrow?

6. We are not the first followers of Jesus to have this problem.

7. Our lack of concern for questions about enough is harming our bodies …

8. and the earth …

9. and our economy …

10. and our communities.

11. We can find hope for all of these questions in communities
    of moral formation shaped by the radical message of the
    gospel.

12. And we can find wholeness in God.

That is basically an overview of the book. The first six chapters
are a bit more wonky, concerned with theological and sociological
questions. It is certainly my hope that I present those questions in
an engaging way, but it seemed such an important place to start.
Those types of questions—things like who do we believe God is,
how do we believe God speaks to us, and what kind of people and
communities might be formed by those beliefs—those are the kinds
of conversations we don't often take time to have in our busy lives.
It is far easier, given all the activities that fill our schedules, to make
assumptions and to never question them. But as followers of the one
who often began his addresses with "you have heard it said … but I
say …," well, it just seems that we should start by asking what it is
we truly believe.

Chapters 7 through 10 are intended to be practical. I will present
some statistics and numbers that may seem at first to be depressing,
but I close each of those chapters with some practices meant to provide hope for living into a new way of thinking.

In the final two chapters I will seek to be hopeful and pastoral,
and provide encouragement for you on this journey.

A few other items I should clear up before we launch into the
book. First, as I stated earlier, I have taken the position of a Christian
speaking to Christians. I have the privilege of speaking to lots of
different people with belief systems different than my own, and I

think those are very important conversations. But that is not what is happening here. So, when I use the word *God*, I am talking about the God of Abraham, Isaac, and Jacob, and the God revealed in the person of Christ. I am referring to the God affirmed in the historic creeds of the church.

Thanks for taking the time to join in this conversation with me. I hope it benefits both of us.

People Consumed by Stuff

One day Jesus was walking down Main Street on his way out of town, and a rich and influential young lawyer came up to him and asked him: "Good Teacher, what must I do to inherit eternal life?"

And Jesus replied, "Give what you can to the synagogue. Ten percent is a good rule of thumb, but whatever you do, don't be a legalist about it. And make sure you have enough left over to contribute to the economy. You know, 'Give to Caesar …'"

And the man went away very happy, because that was exactly what he was already doing.

✦

There are over one hundred brands of deodorant at my grocery store. I counted.

I have ADD—attention deficit disorder. One person recently described the disorder as hearing five different television sets going off in your head, all at once.[1] And, with each American viewing over thirty thousand different media messages a day,[2] myself included, those five TVs in my head are all blaring, **"Buy something."**

My main goal in seeking out deodorant at the grocery store was simply to not smell bad. I didn't really want to smell *like* anything—I just didn't want to smell. But the deodorant aisle was an attention-deficit nightmare. I found seventeen different choices of unscented deodorant alone: different colors, different names, different claims to keep me from sweating, or block odor, or to last long. Lord, have mercy.

And I really mean that—*Lord, have mercy.* I was never really allowed to use phrases like that growing up. I guess it sounded too much like blasphemy. But that little prayer has become part of my inner dialogue. It is a great shorthand call for the divine in places where things seem to have gone amok. Like the deodorant aisle at my grocery store.

Lord, have mercy. In Latin it is *Kyrie Eleison.* This is the start of a prayer the Christian church has uttered for most of her life. And we need God's mercy in this time. How have we come as a culture to need more than one hundred choices of deodorant? And deodorant is hardly the least of our problems.

We seem to have made a mess of things. As I write this, our economy is hung over from an orgy of spending brought about by cheap money financed by rising home prices and government spending. Gasoline for our cars is approaching four dollars a gallon. Costco has a limit on the number of bags of rice shoppers can buy per day because of a global shortage. Thousands of children will die around the globe tonight from what Jeffrey Sachs calls "stupid" hunger—something easily preventable. Lord, have mercy.

Is there enough for everyone? This is an important economic question, and in our discussion here I am certainly going to try to address the question from an economic perspective. But it is not just an economic question, is it? In fact, the question of whether there are sufficient resources in this world may be one of the most important theological questions of our time. How we answer it reveals much regarding our belief about the character of God: who we think God is, how we think God provides for the creation, and what role humans play in that work—this all relates directly to our understanding of God.

In this book I hope to narrate two distinct visions. The first is a vision of people and communities whose lives are out of whack and who are consumed by stuff. Our view of God and our understanding of the way we participate in God's work in the world have become distorted, and we have transformed ourselves into unthinking consumers of products, ideas, and cultural narratives about what will bring us happiness.

The second is a view of people and communities who are guided, and even made more whole, by a vision of God and God's work in the world by which they are consumed. Our decisions regarding what resources and how many of those resources we use are not rooted in oversimplified categories of "more or less," but instead are nourished by a story of a God who is sufficient, active in the world, and forming a community of co-laborers to manage the created order.

The differences between these two views—consumed by stuff and a community consumed by a holistic vision of God's sufficiency—are not simply practical distinctions. I will not, here in these pages, advocate a life lived in balance, or a vision of people and communities consumed by God because it helps proselytize for Christianity. And I am not advocating a life lived in balance because it lowers our electric bills. These differences have an impact on the very story we tell—the story about God, the work of Christ, and what it means to be a follower of Jesus.

I am also not talking about two different stories that can be neatly separated. We do not choose one over the other. Instead, we live somewhere between these two understandings. My prayer in writing these words is that you would become more and more consumed by the vision of a God who is enough, and that you would move more and more toward communities shaped by this vision.

But at some point in a book about consumption, we need to talk about stuff. *Stuff* is a word I am going to employ often through these pages. I use it as a kind of shorthand for the things that gunk up our lives, things that make our lives more complicated without making us more whole. Stuff is also used as a kind of shorthand for a perspective of people and communities who are more characterized by consuming than by being consumed by God. This allows us to speak of the concept without having to reference big, long explanations each time.

Without taking too great a definitional detour, perhaps I should also pause here and talk about what I mean by the word *consume*. That is another word that will receive a lot of ink on these pages, and it is never safe to assume that you and I hold the same definitions for the words we use. And what do we do with all the other words, like *consumption* and *consumerism*? Well, let me shoot off a few quick definitions before we move on:

- *Consume:* to use something. This can be good or bad, and depends on the context.

- *Consumption:* the act of using something. This, too, can be good or bad, depending on the context.
- *Consumerism:* a way of thinking about stuff that believes the consumption of things—food, cars, ideas in books, new models of church—is what will really, *finally* make us content. This is always a bad concept.

THE STORY OF STUFF

So let us speak, then, of stuff.[3] How much do we consume? Why do we consume so much? What hole in our lives are we attempting to fill? And is consumption just about the products we buy at Wal-Mart?

The answer to the first question, "How much do we consume?" is an easy one—we consume *more than at any time in history*. It is rare when we get to make such a bold historical statement. But the simple fact is that we are in a time of unprecedented buying of things, consumption such as has never been before.

In 2003 nearly 50 percent of American household expenditures were for "nonnecessity" items. Compare this to the 21 percent of nonnecessity spending in 1901 and 35 percent of nonnecessity spending in 1960.[4] We are spending more than ever as a nation on items we don't need, but we sure do want. In 2004 American consumers spent $2.2 trillion on entertainment, and $782 billion of that on televisions, radios, and sound equipment.[5] In 2005 we spent $86 billion on sporting goods, including $852 million on snowmobiles and $338 million on archery equipment.[6] (Archery equipment? Really? Who saw that one coming?) Every year we spend more and more on products and services created by our "growing" economy.

Typically when we mention these kinds of statistics, people usually push back by asking, "Well, aren't we making more money now as well? Can't we afford to spend money on things we don't need?" Ah—I thought you would never ask.

Even in a time of income growth, we still spend more than we make. In 2006 the American savings rate was negative for the entire year, the worst rate since the Great Depression. According to one article, "The Commerce Department is reporting that the savings rate for all of 2006 was a negative 1 percent, meaning that overall consumers were dipping into their savings or increasing their borrowing during the year."[7]

Ironically, the same report shows a 0.7 percent increase in personal income. Translation: Even when we increase our income, we still spend more than we have. This is not just a problem that can be solved by tweaking our systems. Something deep within our souls longs for more stuff.

And, there does seem to be evidence we are spending ourselves into a corner we may have great difficulty getting out of. I will cover the economic ramifications of this issue in more detail in chapter 9, but as I write these words in the spring of 2008, the American economy seems headed for a significant correction of the kind that will challenge many of our notions about how much we can spend on things we don't need for daily living.

WHY ALL THIS STUFF?

But merely explaining the history of global consumption does not help us understand why we devour stuff at such massively disproportionate levels. What is it deep within our souls that causes us to want what we do not have and to have what we do not want?

Perhaps we could look to the story of the fall of humanity for some guidance. It seems a logical place to start, since it comes "in the beginning" of the biblical narrative, way back in the early part of the book of Genesis. And this is one of the most fundamental stories within the Judeo-Christian understanding of the world.[8]

Adam and Eve were living in an idyllic world where all their needs were met, including the need to converse in physical space with the God of creation. They did not know what it would be like to want for anything, according to the story. They didn't even know enough to feel goofy walking around a garden in their birthday suits.

But, as you likely know, all this came crashing down when they decided to eat from "the fruit from the tree that is in the middle of the garden" (Gen. 3:3 ESV). They had all that they could possibly need, but they wanted more than what they needed. They wanted what they could not attain without a breach in the relationship between God, humanity, and the created order.

And that breach is the end of the story of the fall, the great moral lesson. Adam and Eve leave the garden. Humanity toils to produce crops among the thorns. We groan in labor pains to ensure a future for this planet and for we travelers who live on it. This story, this story of the fall is, indeed, a "story we find ourselves in."[9] It can and should be a guiding narrative as we ask questions about why we consume so much. The struggles identified in that narrative are as current as this morning's *Wall Street Journal*.

Something deep within us, from time immemorial, causes us to want what we do not have. The desire for more drove colonial expansion by Western nations into new territories, causing us to commit unimaginable atrocities against various races and ethnicities. The desire for more was at the heart of American expansion from a few trading companies and religious colonies out to thirteen colonies and eventually to all of what we consider the United States. In the process of this growth we stole land, abused people, and trampled on many of the rights in our constitutional documents.

But we do not have to look to some grand arc of history, or even to government statistics, to understand the effect of our consumption. In my research regarding the plights and problems of folks in Appalachia I see this firsthand. Men and women are stuck with a coal economy that is devastating their job base and leaving little hope for their future. Children are leaving Appalachia in record numbers, crushing families, some of whom have lived in that area for more than two hundred years. Throughout the coal-mining areas of Appalachia, in almost biblical proportions, neighbor is pitted against neighbor, friend against friend (Isa. 19:2). One family fights to preserve ancestral lands from being taken and blown up to get at the coal seams below, while another enjoys ATVs and a new widescreen TV.

ALL KINDS OF "STUFF"

But stuff is not just products we buy at the store, is it? Perhaps one of the biggest areas of consumption these days is information and ideas. We live in a time of a networked information economy. Each day, thousands of new Web pages are added to the Internet. In 1995 there were eighteen thousand Web sites; in 2006 we crossed the one hundred million Web site mark.[10] This does not even begin to account for the huge rise in blogs, podcasts, videos, and other information finding its way onto the Web.

Some of this is quite good and needed. You may have even heard about this book over the Web, or on some blog tour, or through a podcast. Enabling technologies have given people a voice in business and culture in ways that would have been unimaginable a short time ago. New relationships and conversations are springing up around the globe. New movements are emerging and bringing about change as individuals feel empowered to take charge of their lives, and to do so now rather than wait for someone else to take the lead. As the ninety-fifth thesis of the *The Cluetrain Manifesto* states, "We are waking up and linking to each other. We are watching. But we are not waiting."[11]

Technology saved my faith in a very real way. In the late 1990s I took a few seminary courses at an extension campus of a fairly conservative seminary. A professor there had me read the work of a missionary writer named Lesslie Newbigin, who wrote about how the actions of our churches interpret for the world the message of the gospel. This caused me to weep. I looked at the churches of which I had been a part and was convinced that if people only knew that congregation, knew me, then their understanding of the life and work of Christ would be distorted, at best. I looked at the political captivity of the church to a fairly narrow agenda defined mostly by private sexual activity, and I felt shocked at my role, small though it was, in creating that dynamic.

But what was I to do with these new questions I was asking? I did not know anyone else who was asking the same questions as I. And based on my upbringing, the whole thing felt a little heretical, frankly.

I really felt alone. Lisa thought I was losing my mind. My Christian friends thought I was going to ditch my faith. My Republican friends thought I was going soft. Was I becoming that most horrible of all creatures: a liberal?

So I did what all modern people do when they want to have a conversation—I started a blog.

That seems silly in retrospect. But I did not know where else to turn. And soon I found a community of people who were asking the same questions. I discovered other bloggers writing questions I had only thought in my mind and would never dare type onto a keyboard or ask out loud. I found reviews of books asking, in print, the same questions. I came into relationship with so many people looking for an authentic way to follow God in the way of Jesus, and I came into conversations happening among people seeking to be faithful to this way. During some very dark years, those conversations happening on the Web and in books about God's emergent work in the world kept me from ditching the whole of Christianity.

But it also helped to contribute to my "infoholic" tendencies. I am addicted to information. Google News is a kind of drug for me, and Facebook, well, don't even get me started. What has been so generative in my life—the unedited flow of conversation, thoughts, and new ideas made possible by the unmediated global technology network—also has the possibility to swallow me whole.

And I am not alone. As a culture we are consumed by information: news, insights, opinions; heck, even the weird reality of everyday life. If I had told someone fifty years ago that there would be a show about two wives swapping places for a week, or an entire series about an incompetent hotel heiress acting normal (well, normal for her anyway) in surreal settings, they would have told me I was nuts.

Every year programming executives try to think of brand-new, never-before-thought-of ideas. This should also come as no surprise. But has this made us more whole? Or has it, rather, strengthened a kind of individualism made possible by *The Gutenberg Galaxy*, that world created by technology that provides the new, the not yet thought of, the innovative, the better?

In fact, the statistics I used earlier—that we see thirty thousand media messages a day—is a drastic jump from less than ten years ago when we saw *only* three thousand a day. We now have a historic level of choice over what to buy, what to believe, and how to act. But has this made us more moral or more whole?

Communities Consumed by God

One day Jesus was walking down Main Street on his way out of town, and a rich and influential young lawyer came up to him and asked him: "Good Teacher, what must I do to inherit eternal life?"

And Jesus replied, "Become a better you. Awaken to your life's purpose. Be a people person. Eat what I would eat. And vote right."

And the man went away very happy, because that sounded exactly like the kind of life he had been seeking.

G. K. Chesterton once famously quipped, "Christianity has not been tried and found wanting; it has been found difficult and not tried." This continues to be true today.

Christianity includes an implicit call to embody our faith, to *be* that which we say we believe. In this sense, we are to live *eucharistically*. The Eucharist is a celebration of thanks for all that God, through Christ, has done for us. It is a concept rooted in the idea of celebrating the gracious offering of Christ's life and death. Imagine the transformation in our lives, our communities, our congregations, if we began to literally offer ourselves as "living sacrifices," and did so graciously.

It is also a model that helps us remember the very real and physical aspects of the life and death of Christ. And as all Christ-followers are called to be like our teacher, we must remember that this implies a willingness to truly, not just figuratively, lay down our lives for the other. This notion—gratefully being willing to go to the cross for the unknown, the ungrateful, the outsider, the foreigner—is, I would suggest, the type of Christ following that Chesterton was referring to, the Christianity that has been found difficult and not tried.

MORAL, THERAPEUTIC DEISM

In place of the radical call to eucharistic lives, we have been offered a number of low-cost, low-commitment substitutes. One of these substitutes is what Christian Smith calls "moral, therapeutic deism."[1] This is a phrase he and Melinda Denton used to describe the contemporary spiritual beliefs of American teenagers. According to the authors, here are the basic tenets of this belief:

1. A God exists who created and orders the world and watches over human life on earth.
2. God wants people to be good, nice, and fair to each other, as taught in the Bible and by most world religions.
3. The central goal of life is to be happy and to feel good about oneself.

4. God does not need to be particularly involved in one's life except when he is needed to resolve a problem.

5. Good people go to heaven when they die.[2]

And where might these kids have gotten this notion of a detached, moral, therapeutic God? They got that idea from us, of course. You only need to travel as far as your local Christian bookstore to find this theological worldview. Or you can turn your browser toward Amazon.com, or the untold number of Web sites offering this vision. An entire industry is built on the financial formula of selling books to people that help them have a better sex life, unlock the secrets to their inner desires, understand the masculine/feminine mind, lose weight, and find their purpose in life. Few of these books, and even fewer of the bestsellers, tell of the God who interrupts, engages, and calls us to sacrifice. Does this describe a life gratefully lived in sacrifice for others?

I totally understand the irony of this line of thinking: a guy writing a Christian book attacking the industry that printed and sold the book. You may have bought this at Amazon.com while searching for a Christian perspective on consumerism, or perhaps you heard about it and ordered the book through your local Christian bookstore. That is great. I am not suggesting there is something inherently wrong with Christian bookstores, Christian publishing houses, or Christian television networks. I am merely suggesting that the books we offer, the ideas we promote, need to be *Christian*, they need to offer a call to a life distinctively shaped by the life, death, and resurrection of Jesus Christ.

There is a kind of healing that can come within people and communities following Christ. Our concepts of what is moral and how

God views these choices, are definitely ideas we should strive to define and articulate. But moral theology cannot be formed outside of the community of faith. These begin in The Way, as the early church called herself. It is a kind of gain that can only come from losing our life.

CIVIL RELIGION

But the theology of moral, therapeutic deism is not the only phony substitute offered for the radical call in the gospel to gratefully take up our cross and follow Christ. Another oft-offered counterfeit to the eucharistic life is civil religion. This is the notion that God's primary concern is our nation and our national interests. It is the temptation to see what God is doing in the world and what America is doing in the world as the same thing.

In America this view gained particular importance during the Cold War and the fight against Communist expansion. Communism was an atheistic world system, and thus was rightly perceived to be a threat to Christianity. After all it was Karl Marx, one of Communism's most prominent thinkers, who offered the following thoughts: "Religion is the sigh of the oppressed creature, the heart of a heartless world, just as it is the spirit of an unspiritual situation. It is the opium of the people."

It's interesting that the church's greatest pushback to that statement was regarding the belief that religion was an "opiate," a drug to dull our senses and allow us to be taken advantage of by capitalist marauders. Very rarely did we hear the church object to the notion of "religion as the spirit of an unspiritual situation." We did not seem to mind that Marx criticized our need for spirituality, but calling us irrational—that did it.

I am not pretending there wasn't a very real threat to our safety as a nation during those years. The Second World War brought about a massive shift in American understanding of the world and our place in it. After the decades of expansion driven by the narrative of evolutionary human progress, American soldiers in Hitler's Europe had witnessed firsthand the atrocity and wholesale slaughter of an ethnic group made possible by technological advances. As one writer who died in the gas chambers put it, many dreams died in the fires of Auschwitz.

The Cold War further necessitated shifts in our view of the world. While there had certainly been times during world history when two major superpowers fought for the dominance of the known world, the stakes had never been so high. The atomic bombs dropped on Hiroshima and Nagasaki forever transformed each possible skirmish, each air-raid drill, each move of Communist expansion into a possible precursor for a war that could not only end all wars, but could potentially end all civilization.

We, the American church, also held an understanding that America as a Christian nation was deeply threatened. What would become of what one preacher recently called "the greatest Christian nation in the history of this planet" if it was no longer a nation?

Thus, it was during these Cold War years we also came to believe many things about Christianity that may need to be rethought as we consider this question of what is enough. During that time, in 1954, the words "under God" were added to the Pledge of Allegiance. This was added to cement a notion of America as a

Christian, or at the least a theistic, nation that stood in contrast to the godless Communists. This may have been a needed corrective at the time—I don't know, this was ten years before I was born (but the same year Elvis Presley's first song, "That's All Right," hit the airwaves). But I wonder if, in the intervening years, as we repeat the Pledge over and over again, and teach it to our children, we have come to believe that the actions we as a nation take, or for that matter that anything we as a nation do, are how God would have us act; that "under God" is some kind of implicit statement of blessing, especially when compared with those who are under Allah, or some other understanding than the dominant American conception of God.

This civil religious imitation seemed quite evident during the response to the attacks of September 11, 2001. As I have written about in other places, I was in Washington, D.C., on the day of the attacks. I watched the smoke from the burning Pentagon building plume up over the Potomac. I personally witnessed the looks of terror, shock, amazement, and bewilderment in the eyes of a city gripped by terror. For months afterward, I walked by military tanks on 16th Street guarding the White House. Never in my life would I have imagined soldiers with machine guns patrolling the streets of our nation's capital.

So I have a firsthand understanding of the fear we all faced after that day. We all struggled to understand how these attacks could have happened on our shores. And we all struggled to understand how best to respond. It is in moments of crisis that we tend to default to our learned responses. We allow our most basic instincts to take over and guide us. It is in these times when we most need to look to our principles, our sacred texts, our traditions to allow the wisdom of the past to help guide us in the future.

But we did not choose a response that was rooted in our tradition, or in a life lived in sacrifice. In our response to the terrorist attacks on D.C., New York, and Pennsylvania, the way of peace and reconciliation was not tried and found wanting; it was found difficult and untried. This was even more acutely true in the invasion of Iraq. Ample voices at the time found the invasion of Iraq a rush to judgment, an admission of failure, and a statement of the power of fear to overcome the best in each of us. And yet the notion of God's blessing on our actions was so deeply embedded into our body politic that most never paused to wonder if they were in the right; the church stood in step with the rest of a culture longing for retaliation.

Many voices of leaders from within the church encouraged the rush to war. Jerry Falwell suggested that "God is pro-war." Several leading evangelicals suggested that the invasion of Iraq would open "exciting new doors" for proselytizing Muslims. Tim LaHaye spoke of the invasion of Iraq as "a focal point of end-time events," whose special role in the earth's final days will become clear after invasion, conquest and reconstruction. And, in the clearest statement of civil religion, Charles Stanley offered the following rationale for retaliatory strikes against foreign nations: "God battles with people who oppose him, who fight against him and *his followers*."[3]

Did you notice that? *His followers.* The attacks of September 11 were not on a church or temple. The terrorists did not blow up a Christian school or college. The planes were not flown into a Christian community, or a theological training school like a seminary or divinity school. And yet, in the heart of a time of terror, when a nation struggled to understand how to respond to violence, a renowned preacher and the former head of the Southern Baptist Convention suggested that America, a nation, can join in with God by battling those who attack our country.

WAIT, WEREN'T WE TALKING ABOUT CONSUMERISM?

Right about now you are probably wondering what happened to our conversation about the concept of *enough*. I started with the other concepts of Christianity because I think we need to see the call to live in the model of Christ and the desire to follow in the life and death of Jesus as truly a counterculture and not just some shabby counter to the culture.

In the first vision, the Christian life is just an enhanced version of the life Madison Avenue can offer us. In more militaristic views of Jesus following, we feel stronger, notwithstanding the historic rise and fall of every nation that has ever existed throughout time. But we are most like Christ when we are incarnated in the life of the other.

I fear this idea—living sacrificially, living a life given to others rather than a life of mindless consumption—is constantly being crowded out by cheap knockoffs. Moral, therapeutic deism and civil religion—these are among the low-cost, low-commitment substitutes we have been offered in Christianity that take the place of a eucharistic and sacrificial life; these crowd out the radical call of Christ to take up our cross and follow him. In their place I wish to offer a vision of a eucharistic community.

First, we are to each individually live a eucharistic life. This implies a life of sacrifice. But sacrifice for whom? To be shaped and molded into the image of Christ is to give of oneself to the other, and, perhaps most importantly, to the other who is of a different worldview than yourself. Jesus certainly demonstrated this during his life. The story of the woman at the well recorded in John's gospel is but one example. Jesus took water from a woman who was not only non-Jewish, but had a nasty reputation for sleeping around. His followers were appalled. Jesus was nonplussed. This was exactly the kind of life, a life freely given to others, that he was seeking to demonstrate for his followers.

Jesus was seeking to make that kind of radical welcome normal for those who would be his disciples. This is, I believe, what Jesus was trying to convey as recorded later on in John's gospel account: "I have set you an example that you should do as I have done for you. The truth, I tell you, no servant is greater than his master, nor is a messenger greater than the one who sent him. Now that you know these things, you will be blessed if you do them" (John 13:15–17).

We are quite happy to accept phony substitutes that do not require the same level of sacrifice. But they cannot satisfy us. Just like the woman at the well in John 4, we thirst for that which is of God.

In the American church a challenge to the idea of individuals living eucharistically is the problem of exceptionalism. We read of people who give their lives on behalf of the poor, people who give up money and prestige to move to places that have been abandoned in our system of "progress." And what do we say, at least to ourselves, when we read these accounts? I am so glad *they* are doing that.

We often do ministry by proxy, something the American church pioneered during the nineteenth and twentieth centuries.

But we are to live into the model of Christ in our persons, what-ever our circumstances. To be willing to give ourselves—our resources, our talents, our dreams and aspirations—for the other is to be incarnated in their lives, to be willing to become a disciple to the logical conclusion. It is, quite literally, to share in the body and blood of Christ.

But, like the Communion Supper of bread and wine, the body is not simply a composite of parts. The body of Christ is, in this sense, truly *emergent*, a word that has taken on all manner of meaning, both good and bad, in the contemporary church. Most simply, it conveys the idea that the whole cannot be explained by, or is more than, the sum of its parts.

When we come to the eucharistic meal, we do not partake of flour, baking soda, salt, and yeast. We break bread, or perhaps unleav-ened bread without yeast, but we recognize that it is comprised of those original ingredients and yet has become one element. We do not pass around grapes. We pour wine or juice, which comes from the original fruit and yet has been transformed into something new, something that still shares the original DNA of the fruit and yet is much more.

In the same way, we are called to be the body of Christ. We have many parts, but those parts find their place in the whole. As Paul wrote: "For as in one body we have many members, and the members do not all have the same function, so we, though many, are one body in Christ, and individually members one of another" (Rom. 12:4–5 ESV). To truly live eucharistically is to find ourselves in a community of others seeking the same, seeking to follow God in the way of Jesus.

Sometimes as postmodern people, we stay away from metaphors of wholeness. Perhaps because of backlash against the power used poorly by our religious upbringings or our political systems, we are afraid of any all-encompassing metaphor like the body. But, the gospel is all encompassing. It is inherently a totalizing narrative. To say otherwise is just silly. The gospel is an attempt to explain the whole cosmological narrative through the life, death, and resurrection of the God-man Jesus Christ.

The question, then, becomes what we do with this story. How are we to be shaped by this narrative? This is again where the Eucharist becomes such a helpful metaphor. In the same way that Christ offered his life up for others, he calls us to do the same. We are to live in gratitude, always willing to sacrifice for the other, always willing to give up our power for the other. Imagine a community like that.

3

My God Is So Big

One day Jesus was walking down Main Street on his way out of town, and a rich and influential young lawyer came up to him and asked him: "Good Teacher, what must I do to inherit eternal life?"

And Jesus replied, "Great question! I've never thought of that before. Give me some time to get back to you on that one."

And the man went away pleased, because he really wasn't ready for any big changes at this point in his life.

This conversation we're having here is not really a new one, is it? In fact, as I was writing this book, I noticed a lot of books on the shelves dealing with consumerism, contentment, and eucharistic living.

The notion of the sufficiency of God is not exactly a new topic either. If you grew up in the American church, chances are you sang a song with words like this: "My God is so BIG, so strong and so mighty, there's nothing my God cannot do." These familiar words from the Sunday school song remind us that we have a notion of a big God, one that can meet any need.

So, if the sufficiency of God is something so simple even a child can understand it, why are there so many books on the subject? I suspect one of the reasons is that we continue to have really warped constructs of God. In *Justice in the Burbs*, Lisa and I talked about the need for a new view of God, one that was rooted in Scripture and the tradition of the church. For questions of living justly, this is important in that we have largely perceived God as insufficient or unconcerned with our actions, and we've acted that way. We suspect the same is true of our understanding about actions and beliefs about consumption.

Somewhere, deep within each of us, is an understanding about God. We don't often use the word *theology* when talking about issues of everyday living, but somehow we need to find a means to bring a discussion of our understanding of God into the conversation about consumption. We suspect that at the root of many of the causes that drive us to overconsume is a view that God and God's creation is insufficient to meet our needs, or a view that God is so distant from the concerns about our daily lives that he is unconcerned about our levels of consumption.

You might ask, "Are we really so aware of our beliefs about God that we can say our understanding is shaped by them?" Well, yes and no. I don't believe most of us are aware of our beliefs about God. We all hold some big-picture understandings of who God is and how God is at work in the world, and we think about them on Sundays or when hanging out with friends from church.

But we do hold other understandings about God than just the big ones, right? Take, for example, the use of energy. When we use energy without thought of consequence it seems that we are making one of two theological statements. Either we believe that the resources of creation are given to us without concern for their stewardship, or we believe that God is unconcerned with how we use the resources we have been given. Neither of those views seems consistent with what we can learn about God from Scripture or the tradition of the church.

Consider the story of manna as told in the Hebrew books of Exodus and Numbers. The people of Israel were complaining, wishing they had chosen to stay in the slave camps of Egypt rather than wander through the barren desert. In the story, God provides daily food for the wanderers in the form of *manna*, which means "what is it?" proving that even the writers of the Pentateuch had a sense of humor.

We can learn something about the character of God from this story of provision. When people were in need, God provided. It seems that this lesson could be more broadly applied throughout the realm of resources we find in this world to demonstrate that, in the creation, there is always enough for what we need.

But we learn about more than God's sufficiency in the story of the manna. We also learn about the proper use of resources. In the story the people were not content to gather manna each day. Here is what happened: "And Moses said to them, 'Let no one leave any of it over till the morning.' But they did not listen to Moses. Some left part of it till the morning, and it bred worms and stank" (Ex. 16:19–20 ESV).

In other words, this story is not just about God's provision, but it deals with the way in which we are expected to use those resources. Not only was God sufficient to meet their needs, but also God, speaking through Moses, had a view for how those resources were to be used.

How might we apply this story to questions of consumption? It seems as if, all too often, we get caught up in interpretation issues—did this really happen, and how did this story come to us? But perhaps this is where the role of the church in delivering Scripture to us is so important. The preservation of the Bible is part of the work of the church through the ages, including the inclusion of these books and this story. So, while we see this story as rooted in the character of God, we also believe it relates to the story God's people, both Hebrew and Christian, have been telling about God for millennia.

A similar story appears in the gospel of John. Jesus has fed thousands of people with five loaves and two fishes. Does this sound like a familiar theme? Jesus certainly thought so. When the people heard that Jesus was near, they raced to catch up with him, anxious for another miracle. "Rabbi, when did you come here?" (John 6:25 ESV) they asked, looking for some more Jesus magic. Jesus replies, "Very truly, I tell you, you are looking for me, not because you saw signs, but because you ate your fill of the loaves" (John 6:26). In other words, their view of God extended about as far as their stomachs.

THE DEATH OF [GOD]

But even that God—the God who fills hungry bellies, who calms the storm, who heals the leper—that God has been on the outs in the rational Western world for some time. Sure, that God still shows up at homeless shelters and urban missions, and is desperately hoped for at exam time or when we are overdue for our quarterly report. But the Enlightenment was not kind to that God. Friedrich Nietzche proclaimed him "dead." Systematic theologians cut him up and labeled every part. And fundamentalists reduced Christianity to a recitation of those parts. Along the way, us non-theologians and nonphilosophers took a more practical approach. We just forgot God. Or, at the least, our actions told that story.

In terms of consumption of the world's resources, America is number one. Woo-hoo! We have about 5 percent of the world's population and consume well over 30 percent of the world's natural resources. We lead the world in per capita consumption of oil, precious metals, and food. Yet, throughout these times, we have never stopped and asked if this was right.

There is a saying in philosophy: Every ought implies a can. In other words, it is assumed that everything we should or ought to do is also something that we have the ability to do. But in America we seem to have turned that equation on its head: Every can implies an ought. We have assumed that because we can build bigger cars, bigger homes, bigger shopping malls, that we ought to do those things. We have acted as if there was nothing in the model of Christ, Scripture, or the tradition of the church that could speak to this issue.

We even built bigger churches and created new means of marketing the gospel. Why? Because we could, and, therefore, we believed we should. This began in earnest in the nineteenth century with people like Charles Finney, who proclaimed: "The Church is dead and lifeless. Preaching that is not immediately practical for people is not good and should not be done."

In my lifetime I have lived through a variety of church growth and evangelism methods: lifestyle evangelism, cell-group ministries, friendship evangelism, seeker sensitivity. I even see a number of churches that have reduced the concept of God's emergent work in the world down to an "emergent" service. All these methods share one common trait, that is, they are methods. They are instructions for the material creation of a desired world. We have become intoxicated with our ability to shape our world, and the God of mystery has suffered.

GOD IN THE GUTENBERG GALAXY

And perhaps we have suffered as well. Another statistic America leads is the number of cases of attention deficit disorder. We are indeed a distracted people.

Marshall McLuhan predicted this distraction in his 1962 book, *The Gutenberg Galaxy*. In that work he predicted the social breakdown that would come from the increase in choices made available by technology. It was not his concern to ask about the theological breakdown from that same increase in technology, but I think this is an important question for the church to ask.

Perhaps you are old enough, like me, to remember when the town you lived in had only one movie theater, showing only one movie at a time. Then came the multiplex theater, with more than one choice. Then came multiple theaters per town. Now I need a complex scheduling matrix to pick the movie and location. And this is all without considering renting movies by mail, downloading them online, or buying them on iTunes. Egads.

And that is just the movies. We have become deluged with a broad array of theological choices in the marketplace of ideas. More and more

worldviews compete for our mind's market share. More and more the-
ologies compete for our attention, even if that theology is no more
complex than helping us eat what Jesus ate. We have too much data,
and are no longer able to make up our minds.

The end result of this multitude of choices is that we tend to pick
the simplest one. This is what Finney realized. During the nineteenth
century in the New World, people suddenly had religious choices
that would have been unimaginable in Western Europe. So rather
than call people to live in eucharistic community, a call that would
require a great deal of sacrifice, Finney invited them to walk down
the aisle and "ask Jesus into their hearts." All that was required was a
simple accedence to the most basic part of the gospel.

This has had significant implications for our theology here in
America. I fear that Jesus has been transformed from the God who
radically and incarnationally engages with the world, to the God
who was around long enough to perform the divine transaction of
our salvation. "God became flesh and dwelt among us," and yet most
of us have given no thought to the lessons we might learn from the
life of Christ, including those lessons that relate to our questions of
sufficiency and contentment.

Now, before you get all in a huff, I am not suggesting there is
not something wonderful and mysterious about the death and resurrection of Christ and the work of Christ to redeem the whole world.
John 3:16–17 is the starting point of my faith, and the means by
which the whole of the world is explained. But I am suggesting that
our cultural and theological attention deficit disorder has caused us
to focus on that single element as the whole of the gospel, and it is
retarding our journey of faith.

Go to your average evangelical church and open the hymnal, or get a list of the worship songs most frequently sung. What is the theme of the overwhelming majority of those songs? The act of salvation. There is a time when the wonder of Christ's work on the cross should bring us to our knees in gratitude. And, it should serve as a constant backdrop for our journey of faith, including the wonder of the simple message "Jesus loves me, this I know," the phrase Karl Barth quoted as the most profound theological truth in his whole lifetime of discovery. But it is not the whole of our journey. The work of Christ on the cross is not even the whole of Scripture. It is the beginning of a new chapter in the story of God, but it is not the finale. Rather the gospel accounts serve, as Phyllis Tickle recently suggested, in the same role as the Pentateuch, forming a framework for our ongoing conversation and struggle to interpret how to live as God's people in the world.

CALLING ALL PROPHETS

Perhaps what we need, then, is a new wave of prophets, people willing to speak God's truth into action in our current world. We are not short on secular prophets—their prophecies of everything from the financial future to the globalized world line the bookshelves of our stores.

But if we are to get back to living in rhythm with God's heartbeat and finding answers to our questions of what is enough, we must find the farmers and shepherds, or in our case, the lawyers and Starbucks baristas and stay-at-home moms or dads, who are willing to speak prophetically as followers of Jesus back into our culture and especially into the church.

Would we recognize them? Who knows? God's people did not always see or hear the prophets, unless they walked naked through the streets. (That wasn't a suggestion, by the way.) How would God speak through the prophets today? What would that sound like? What would prophets look like today?

It seems that we constantly need prophetic reminders, ways of calling ourselves back to the narrative. We need to be reminded, in fresh and contemporary words, what kind of people we are being called to become.

Toward that end, I would like to suggest the following as a possible retelling of Amos 5:18–27. The writings of Amos, an Old Testament prophet, have much to say to us today. He was writing at a time when material pleasures had crowded out and overtaken the spiritual devotion of the people of Israel. He decried the emptiness of their devotion and called God's people to move beyond nominal devotion to Yahweh. Amos condemned the people for getting rich while not taking care of their workers. He spoke out against the problems farmers were facing. Sound familiar?

Feel free to go read the original verses right now, and then come back for the following recasting of God's voice to today's American church:

GOD, SPEAKING TO THE AMERICAN CHURCH:

You spend too much time thinking about and wishing for the end of the world. Why are you so anxious to bring about God's judgment? And what kinds of people have you become, thinking the world will end tomorrow?

In your arrogance and laziness you have forgotten why I placed you here. You have endless conferences and seminars on "how to do church," but you have forgotten to be the church, a people who faithfully live as an alternative community, pointing all people toward me through loving service.

You have grown rich exploiting the poor. You bring a tiny pittance of that money back to me and say, "God, You have been so good to us." But your money smells like crap in my nostrils. It sickens me and I don't want it. Give it back to the poor from which it came.

You grow more food than you need by destroying the very soil I gave you to tend. You sit down to a sumptuous buffet and say, "Look how God has blessed us." I have not blessed you. I have left you to your own destruction.

There will come a day when the womb of the earth will no longer produce and the poor will rise up and pledge never to sew a cheap garment again. You will grow hungry and your shopping malls will close. Then you will turn to me and cry, "God, why have you rejected us?" And I will say, "I have not rejected you. I have been here all along, waiting for your return."

So turn your face toward me now. Seek after me. Live out my commands. Do you want to be people after my own heart? Then care for the poor, the needy, the marginalized, those for whom my heart has always beat loudly. Cease your endless Bible studies, searching for the answer to righteous living. Commit yourselves to following what I already told you to do. Don't believe you are pursuing me if you are not seeking to do justice.

Care for the planet. You have become so worried about who might also advocate this course of action that you forgot it was one of my first commandments to you. Tend well what I have given you.

Seek the welfare of your community. As people in exile, your future and the future of the place you live are one and the same. So make your world more whole, that you might be more holy.

And live in love. I had hoped you would get that message when my Son joined humanity and demonstrated sacrificial love in action. But you are so worried about his return that you forget why he came. Be a people shaped by the model of Jesus, not just the prospect of escaping the world I have asked you to help heal.

4

Flannelgraph Jesus

One day Jesus was walking down Main Street on his way out of town, and a rich and influential young lawyer came up to him and asked him: "Good Teacher, what must I do to inherit eternal life?"

And Jesus replied, "Don't marry someone of the same gender, and don't allow someone you have gotten pregnant to have an abortion."

And the man went away very happy, because he was already doing those things.

Our contemporary models of moral living are really inadequate. Most of our understanding of proper living involves sex: who we can have sex with, when, and what happens if we make a sexual mistake. These are important questions, but they are not the whole ball of wax.

And yet these are often the first lessons of morality we learn, and also often the only substantive talk about morality we get from our parents and offer to our children. Sure, your mom tried to guilt you with the starving kids in Africa to get you to eat your peas. But did you ever get a special talk from your parents about hunger in the developing world, something akin to the famous (or infamous, depending on your parents) "sex talk," where they awkwardly explain the birds and the bees? How about a coming-of-age discussion about the inequalities of global capitalism? No, huh? Me neither.

I don't want to diminish questions of sexuality. They are deeply rooted in our ideas of enough and sufficiency, and we will spend some more detailed time on those questions later. But I do want us who are followers of Jesus to find a fuller understanding of morality. As disciples of Christ, this understanding can, and should, be rooted in the teachings and life of Christ.

Unfortunately, most evangelical Christians don't seem to know that much about Jesus. I was in college before I heard a sermon from the Gospels that was not either delivered at Christmas or Easter, or was not a sermon asking the people in the audience to "ask Jesus into their hearts," a phrase that, ironically enough, is not in the Gospels, or in the Bible for that matter. No pastor in my formative years preached a whole sermon series in one of the Gospels, the way they did through Romans or Galatians.

So many of us enter adulthood and, despite having grown up in the church, have this childish, flannelgraph version of Jesus. Jesus is a fuzzy cutout figure that sticks to the felt, right under the tree where Zacchaeus is looking down, waiting for Jesus to invite himself over for tea. (Just as an aside, the song "Zacchaeus Was a Wee Little Man," actually ends with the words, "for I'm going to your house today." But, my grandmother was from Scotland and used to sing, "for I'm going to your house for tea," and I still sing it that way.) Sometimes fuzzy Jesus shows up in front of Lazarus's tomb. And flannelgraph Jesus is always at his own tomb, beside the two fuzzy angels who both, as I recall, looked like Fabio and were oddly twin-like.

I guess it is hard to capture the nuances of the life of Christ when you are confined to material that sticks to felt. Baby Jesus is another one of our childish images of the incarnate God. If our prime conception of the God who joined humanity and truly dwelt among us is a baby in a manger, well, I have no idea how that would help me when I am at the mall and trying to buy more responsibly.

But I suspect that our least helpful caricature of the life of the incarnate God is when we focus exclusively on the Jesus of the cross, the tomb, and the resurrection. Thinking back on my childhood, I had a very strange conception of Jesus between the manger and the cross.

In my mind, the Jesus between the manger and the cross was ethereal and wispy and talked in an odd British accent. He would show up from time to time and perform certain miracles, but those were only to let people know that something big was about to happen. They were like the coming attractions at the movie theater. The actual miracles were nothing special; they were merely signposts on the great march to the cross.

In my earliest childhood memories, I imagined Jesus just floating above the earth, like that story in John's gospel about the disciples in the boat. Jesus shows up while they are out in the water and—poof!—they are on the land. I suspected this was just a normal mode of travel for the Savior, like Uncle Arthur in *Bewitched*.

But Jesus was a flesh-and-blood man, with all that implies. He went to the bathroom. He banged his finger with a hammer. He had desires. He grew hungry and thirsty. Jesus was not simply a piece of paper with felt on his back, nor was he simply the man of Easter week, or the baby of Christmas morning. As the writer of the book of Hebrews states it, he became "like his brothers and sisters in every respect" (Heb. 2:17 NRSV). And further down, "Because he himself was tested by what he suffered, he is able to help those who are being tested" (Heb. 2:18 NRSV). So, as we consider what it means to have enough, we are going to spend some time in the life of Christ.

JESUS AND "THE OTHER"

A phrase that gets thrown around a lot these days is *the other*. People, mostly philosophers and theologians, make bold claims about this other. Who exactly is *the other*? In simplest terms, the other is that which is not me. Thinking about the other is a way to examine ourselves in light of the world, and in light of those we connect with on a daily basis. We do not often examine ourselves this way. We do not ask, Who am I?

Here is who I am: I am a middle-aged man of European origin. I was raised in the American Northeast, in New Jersey, which I tell people is a good place to be *from*. I have lived my whole adult life in the American Southeast, mostly in suburban settings. Three years ago I relocated to an urban area.

But those are just the surface-level distinctions. I have lived my whole life as a follower of Jesus—I have never known any other faith tradition. I was educated at quite conservative schools, at least until I began my PhD. So, my thought processes are still bent in the direction of the conservative scholarship in which I was trained. I find that although I shifted my political and theological focus significantly, I still process the big questions of life as a conservative.

But I am also a person of economic privilege. While I never have been wealthy by American standards, I have never known need. At no point in my life have I been marginalized, or more than one or two phone calls away from solving any problem I could create. I have never gone more than a day without food, except by choice. I have never worn old clothes or had to shop at Goodwill, except by choice. My ability to control my destiny is great. Even my move into an urban area of need was facilitated by the power I possess.

Jesus, by contrast, was quite marginalized. He was born a Jew. He was born during a time of Roman control. He was born into a poor, working-class family. Yet his life was characterized by reaching out to the other, to those who were not like him. We all know the stories about the woman at the well and the healing of the lepers. But Jesus displayed the same attitude toward Nicodemus, a wealthy Pharisee, even when he had to sneak in a conversation with Jesus at night so as not to be seen by his peers. Jesus had the same willingness to help the centurion whose appeal to Jesus on behalf of his daughter is captured in Matthew's gospel account. Imagine how scandalous that must have seemed to those who felt oppressed by Roman occupation. By today's standards, it would be as if Jesus helped a member of the Taliban.

The only class of people Jesus seemed to treat as other was the religious zealots. (Whether he really did treat them as other is the subject for another conversation.) And in our contemporary American theological and political dialogue, we have come to behave quite like those zealots. We have come to believe that we must defend ourselves against the other; that the duty of Christ-followers is to believe the right things and adhere to the right models, and to then excoriate those who believe and act otherwise. But this is not to be found in the life of Christ. Against all logic, on the cross Jesus even begs forgiveness for those who are crucifying him. As Richard Kearney has stated, "The very uniqueness of Jesus is the refusal of exclusivity."[1]

As followers of Jesus, we must then ask how this concept of the other might inform our lives. And, in this conversation we are having about stuff, consumption, and enough, we must ask if this idea of the other has anything to say to these questions.

This is made more difficult by the globalization of our economy. Five hundred years ago, if we were to ask questions about the consumption of natural resources, we would assume that most of those resources came from our local area. Even one hundred years ago in the United States over 90 percent of the population was involved in raising their own food. Today that figure is less than 1 percent. We eat asparagus from Brazil, we buy sneakers from Taiwan, and we burn coal from Appalachia. In a globalized world, who exactly is the other?

I will spend some time later on dealing with the specific implications of our globalized economy on questions of consumption and justice. But first we must understand this principle: Jesus cared for the other, and to be a follower of Jesus is to do the same. In one of the most scandalous parables of the gospel, Jesus tells us that he is incarnated, that he is present in a very real and physical way, in the person of those in need. But most of us do not know anyone hungry or thirsty. We do not know someone without clothing or in prison. No strangers come to our door to be welcomed in. Who, then, is the other?

JESUS AND SUSTAINABILITY

Another surprising aspect of the life of Christ was his work toward the restoration of the physical. As Robert Farrar Capon notes, every miracle of Jesus except one, the cursing of the fig tree, was a miracle of the restoration of the creation.[2] Jesus healed lepers and cast out demons; he even turned water into wine.

Jesus knew his time on the earth was short. He seemed to know from the beginning of his ministry that he would not be on this planet for a long time. Yet he still participated in restoring the cosmos, the created world that he spoke into being at the start of time.

By contrast, most of us act like tomorrow is a concept we can be unconcerned about. We mindlessly consume energy, food, and products from nonrenewable resources, and throw away that which we do not want or need. But where exactly is *away*?[3] Where is the place to which things travel when we throw them away, never to affect us again?

Here in this country we throw away fifteen billion plastic bottles every year.[4] We even throw away 14 percent of the food each of us buys at the grocery store, and perhaps as much as half of the food we produce gets discarded. That's right: Tons of food each year comes into our kitchens and our restaurants and ends up in the wastebasket.

This seems to run contrary to the model of Christ. Remember the story about the feeding of the multitudes as told in the Gospels.

What happened at the end of that meal? "And all of them ate and were filled; and *they took up the broken pieces left over,* seven baskets full" (Matt. 15:37 NRSV).

I'm sure the gospel writer was also seeking to make a broader point about the abundance of the work of Jesus, but even that fits into our theme of Jesus and enough. Jesus' view of abundance was not about providing much for a few. Nor was his view that of contemporary conservation efforts, which seek to sequester the earth from sustainable employment of resources. Instead, Jesus seemed concerned with *sustainability,* which is shorthand for the attitude we are to embody that we expect that there will be a world tomorrow, and we are to live and act accordingly.

One of the least sustainable aspects of American culture is the way and the rate at which we incarcerate people into federal and state prisons. Today, in the land of the free, we have 5 percent of the world's population and 25 percent of the world's prisoners.[5] It seems that of all the things we throw away, people are at the top of the list.

One in eight of all adult African American males in this country are behind bars.[6] All across this nation prison corporations, businesses that run houses of incarceration, sell prisons as a means of economic development for depressed rural areas. State legislators fight for the contracts to allow prisons to be placed in the rural communities of their state. As Alan Elsner talks about in his book on the American prison system, *Gates of Injustice,* multigenerational prisoners are becoming the norm. We now have fathers and sons serving sentences in the same prisons. *Lord, have mercy.*

In situations like this I am not sure how helpful it is to ask questions like "What would Jesus do?" because it is difficult to imagine how Jesus would legislate if he were a state senator from a rural district in the twenty-first century. But we can ask, Is this consistent with Jesus? And when we remember that Jesus was the one who burst onto the scene proclaiming "freedom for the oppressed," we can quite safely say that our policy of throwing away people is not resonant with the life and model of Christ.

Ironically, the incarceration rate has spiked during the time when we have focused quite heavily on moral—and perceived Christian—issues in our federal and state elections. We have often reduced the complex issues of morality and of living together in moral community to a few binary issues that then get assigned catchphrases like "pro-life." But, in the words of Sr. Joan Chittister, "There is a big difference between being pro-life and being pro-birth."[7]

JESUS AND LIFE

What does it mean, then, to be proactively for life? Jesus said, "I came that they may have life and have it abundantly" (John 10:10 ESV). But Jesus also said, "a man's life does not consist in the abundance of his possessions" (Luke 12:15), and "life is more than food, and the body more than clothes" (Luke 12:23). And we are told that "those who want to save their life will lose it, and those who lose their life for my sake will save it" (Luke 9:24 NRSV).

So are we are all clear now on the definition of life? I can hear you screaming, No, we're not all clear now!

Another problem we have in taking the life of Christ into context in our situation is that we live in a world where language and concepts have become much more atomized. This is especially true for English speakers, who have more than half a million words at their disposal.[8] We have words like *abundance, fullness, health, strength, vitality*—all of which apply to some aspect of life. For the Hebraic mind, they would have heard many of these concepts in the word *life*.

Thus, for a twenty-first-century follower of Jesus, seeking to live a life modeled after the words of Christ, we must hold several values in tension. First, we need to view life itself, the very beat of our heart and the pulsing of blood through our veins, as connected into God's heartbeat. We have a view of life that is binary: We live, then we die. But we are repeatedly promised the resurrection of our very bodies. Jesus himself ascended into the heavens in his earthly body. These somatic beings that we walk around in have eternal value to the God of the old and new creation. Thus, if the one who dies with the most toys wins, the race can never be won.

What, then, does it mean to lose one's life? That to me is the heart of the gospel—we are to see our lives from the same perspective as God. Without succumbing to an invocation of the metaphysical God, we can nonetheless acknowledge that there is a God who exists outside of our understanding of time and space. There is a God who sees what we cannot or do not see, namely the long-term view of our lives.

And from that perspective, what matters to God? To give oneself to the poor, the hungry, and those in need. Imagine what our own lives would be transformed into if we saw ourselves in the same long view as God. Imagine how we might transform our view of humanity and of care for the creation if we daily reminded ourselves that Christ continues to be incarnated in the flesh.

But related to our discussion here, imagine if we began to transfer our lives into a eucharistic sacrifice to a world in need. If we took the words of Jesus quite literally and were willing "to lay down our lives for our friends." What would change about our communities of faith? What would change about our relationship to our neighbors?

As I suggested earlier, we have been offered relatively low-commitment versions of the radical call to faith. To be "for life" means little more to many Christians than to pull a lever every even year. What would happen to the church, to our towns and cities, to our country, and to our culture if we promoted the complex but abundant view of life presented in Christ?

5

I Wish We'd All Been Ready

One day Jesus was walking down Main Street on his way out of town, and a rich and influential young lawyer came up to him and asked him: "Good Teacher, what must I do to inherit eternal life?"

And Jesus replied, "Sell everything you have and give it to the poor."

And the man replied, "If I just sold everything and gave it to the poor, I can't see where that would advance the gospel as much as I'm doing."[1]

And Jesus walked away, wondering if the man had heard a word he said.

✦

If you were staying in a house that you believed was about to be demolished any day, would you do the dishes or vacuum the floor? And, if you believed that you lived in a world that was about to be destroyed, would you even care when hearing reports about the end of peak oil or the destruction of Appalachia to get at coal seams?

It seems to me that the church in general has a credibility gap on the issues of community and consumption, driven in part by beliefs about the soon return of Christ. This seems more particularly true for a portion of the American evangelical church that spends a lot of time focusing on this issue. Specifically, I wonder if those who have benefited financially from predicting the soon destruction of the world, and then used that money to build things in that world, might cause some to question their message. How might those who are not followers of Jesus and are skeptical about religion perceive this significant breakdown between words and deeds?

For example, one individual whose whole ministry is focused on the end times personally owns a $2.1 million, 7,969 acre ranch with five separate lodges, a caretaker's house, a gun locker, a skeet range, and three barns. Another individual who has made millions writing novels about the soon end of the world has then taken that money and built a hockey rink at a major Christian college.

These huge disparities between words and deeds make for great late-night fodder. They also feed our sense of cynicism, while making it all too easy, sadly, to fail to see the plank in our own eyes. But behind the surface-level analysis, this disparity needs to be seen as part of a larger narrative, one that has a significantly negative effect on our consumption of resources.

The theological view that the world will end soon with the imminent return of Christ is not a new one. Throughout the life of the church this view has had some currency. His return was certainly something Jesus wanted his disciples to believe in and anticipate.

However, it took on a sense of heightened importance in the late nineteenth century. This was at the peak of the Industrial Revolution, when people were looking for something, anything, in the future to explain their pretty miserable present state. I also suspect that the end-times prophetic view gained some interest at the end of the late 1800s as a counter to increases in knowledge and to the release of Darwin's *Origin of the Species*. For many centuries the church had controlled the story of where we came *from*. I have wondered if, as the church lost some control of that story, our present fascination with end-times eschatology became a counter-balance attempt to control the story of where we *are going*.

But what kind of people might be formed by the view of the world as temporal and soon to pass? I remember a comedy from my childhood. I think it was the *Brady Bunch*, but I wouldn't swear to it. Anyway, the kid on the show got five minutes to run through the local toy store with a shopping cart, stuffing products into the cart as quickly as he could.

After watching it, I went to Marco's Playmart, a toy and sporting goods store near my house, and imagined how cool it would be if that were to happen to me. Five minutes to stuff the cart with toys, sports stuff, and gifts, all before the time ran out. I would start with new hockey skates and a new stick. Then I would go for the Chuck Taylor high top sneakers. And a game of Risk—I love that game.

And, well, you get the idea. I remember walking through the aisles of that store like it was yesterday, thinking of all the cool things I would grab if I had only five minutes to take anything I wanted in the store. I remember thinking about the size and shape of different objects, and wondering which should go in first to make sure I would not run out of room before the contest ended.

I fear sometimes that in our rush to convince others, particularly those who are not followers of Jesus, that we know how the world is going to end, we tend to warp our message, and we tend to warp ourselves. I fear that we might see the world like Marco's Playmart, and we believe that the contest is going to end in five minutes.

THE SPIRIT OF THE ANTICHRIST

Listen to what the prophet Jeremiah told God's exiled people:

> "Build houses and live in them; plant gardens and eat their produce. Take wives and have sons and daughters; take wives for your sons, and give your daughters in marriage, that they may bear sons and daughters; multiply there, and do not decrease. But seek the welfare of the city where I have sent you into exile, and pray to the LORD on its behalf, for in its welfare you will find your welfare" (Jer. 29:5–7 ESV).

Translation: This world *is* my home. It is our home. We are not just passing through. This world, the place where we marry and raise families and struggle to make ends meet, this is the location of God's blessing.

We often have a hard time with that concept. Perhaps we see the world as fallen and spoiled. The early church struggled with believing that Jesus could have actually joined with the creation and been formed of the same red clay as comprised God-breathed humanity. But the church roundly condemned the disbelief in the humanity, in the earthbound nature, of Jesus the Messiah.

This very question about the fleshiness of Christ is what John takes on when he says

> "By this you know the Spirit of God: every spirit that confesses that Jesus Christ has come in the flesh is from God, and every spirit that does not confess Jesus is not from God. This is *the spirit of the antichrist*, which you heard was coming and now is in the world" (1 John 4:2–3 ESV).

Did you catch that? The anti-Christ, the opposition to Christ, is the one who denies the incarnation. I remember watching *A Thief in the Night* on a big sheet in my church's parking lot back in the 1970s. For many nights after that I would have frightening dreams about the Antichrist. In the movie he was from the United Nations, I think. Or maybe that was just the announcer, the guy with the black armband that had the Mark of the Beast on it. But in my dreams the Antichrist was Russian, or otherwise from some Communist Bloc nation. He also had a mustache.

I was one of those kids who used to have Left Behind moments. I would come home from school and go through the house calling, "Mom," all while Larry Norman's song "I Wish We'd All Been Ready" was running through my head like a macabre sound track. On more than one occasion during my formative years I burst into tears, convinced that the rapture had occurred and I had been found wanting. Perhaps my sinner's prayer had not stuck. I recall telling this to an audience a few years ago at a theological gathering, and a woman in the crowd blurted out, "Man, that's messed up." Yeah, thanks.

And then one day, well into my adulthood, I did a basic word search on "Antichrist." Try it for yourself at Bible Gateway (www.BibleGateway.com) or any other Bible search engine. Much to my surprise, the word *Antichrist* never appears in the book of the Revelation. Nowhere. Nada. Zip. Despite all the linkage of the end times and the Antichrist, he is nowhere to be found in that mac daddy of all end-times prophecy, John's Revelation.

So, what gives? And I wonder if Tim LaHaye knows this. There are a number of theories on the question of how the word *antichrist* came to be mixed into contemporary end-times prophecy. But I suspect that assigning the Antichrist to some future, evil person is much easier than addressing the issue John was seeking to cover with his use of the term. John wanted to convey the reality that Jesus in fact came in the flesh.

It seems that we are still fighting the battle of the incarnation of Christ, as John was seeking to address in his letter. If this is true, that God became incarnate and entered our world, then that has a whole range of meaning for how we live in the flesh today. If Jesus joined with creation, then that has a whole range of implications for how we think about, live in, and care for, the creation. But if the Antichrist is just a mustached Communist, or now, perhaps, someone from the Middle East, our current bogeyman, then that has less of a call on our daily lives and actions. That is for some time in the future.

How can, and should, this understanding affect the way we view the resources of this earth? And, will we pause long enough from our fear and anxiety about the affairs of the world to answer that question? Because it seems that, just like at the peak of the Industrial Revolution, we now live in uncertain and troubling times. A renegade band of terrorists flew jets into our totems of economic and military might, the World Trade Towers and the Pentagon. With that as a partial justification, we invaded a sovereign nation unprovoked. Daily news from Iraq floods in, and most of it is bad.

We have infected spinach and mad-cow-diseased beef in our grocery stores. Global warming, vaccination fears, school shootings—the list goes on and on. We have no shortage of things to be troubled about in these times. And those fears certainly make the end of this world, with all its troubles and cares, a most appealing proposition.

SAMSON'S WAGER

I want to suggest that hoping for the end of the world is, at the least, not a good wager. Nearly four hundred years ago, the French philosopher Blaise Pascal suggested several arguments that present a way of thinking about the existence of God as a kind of safe bet. This is his famous wager that many of us learned about in philosophy class. Pascal's wager stated simply that, although the existence of God can never be proven from a scientific perspective, belief in God is the safest gamble. It has the better odds. If you are wrong and there is nothing after you exit this planet, then your religious beliefs have given you a life filled with purpose and meaning. And if you are right, Pascal argued, you escape the fires of hell and enjoy God forever.

I am going to suggest a similar wager to you now. For nearly two thousands years, within the church, two things have been true: (1) we are to expect the soon return of Jesus Christ; and (2) we are to work until he comes.

In light of that, here is the gamble I am going to propose: It is just as safe a bet that the return of Jesus will not happen for five hundred years, one thousand years, or even more, as that it will happen tomorrow. If history is our guide, then we will do well to begin asking what kind of world we will leave for our children, grandchildren, and future generations, and adjusting the way we live in the world accordingly. But I fear that in our rush to imagine the end of the world, including scooping up endless copies of the Left Behind books, we have failed to imagine our place in a world that could continue on for a very long time.

Study after study shows that the average Christian in America is statistically indistinguishable from someone of another faith, or of no faith. The culture seems to have an attitude of "eat, drink and be merry, for tomorrow we die," and we join in the party. But is this the correct posture for a follower of Jesus?

REIMAGINING READINESS

I want us to reimagine, and to renarrate, this idea of wishing we'd all been ready, and suggest that the possibility of a future for this earth is the very thing for which we should be ready, and one of the very things for which we will be judged. We have been given the earth as stewards, much like the servants in the parable of the talents found in Matthew 25. Yet we spend very little time imagining, thinking creatively, about how we might steward and enhance this resource.

Instead, we seem—or at least the loudest among us seem—to be narrating a story of the soon end of the earth. While this may happen—the church throughout her life has certainly held to the soon return of Christ—we have lost our way by making this the dominant story. In the wake of this tale we have allowed all manner of atrocities to occur.

We must also renarrate our place on this earth as followers of Jesus. We must find our way back into a story that resonates with the teachings of Christ and the history of the church. In our look to the future we have forgotten both the past and the present. In this way, we have, quite ironically, been captive to the story of evolutionary human progress as told in modernity. This is especially true for us Protestants. We have sought to tell the story that the past has no claim on us, and the future is outside of our control. This has caused us to not be conscious of our indebtedness to the past or our role in the creation of the future.

6

The Eucharist and the Social Construction of Theology

As a contrast to being ready for the soon destruction of the planet, I want to narrate a different end goal for us. Throughout the New Testament, one word is used quite frequently, and that is the Greek word *telos*. For example, this word shows up when Paul says, "It is he [Christ] whom we proclaim, warning everyone and teaching everyone in all wisdom, so that we may present everyone mature in Christ" (Col. 1:28 NRSV). That word translated "mature" is from the Greek word *telos*.

Teleological concerns, then, have to do with the goal we are trying to reach. When we use phrases like "begin with the end in mind," one of Stephen Covey's *Seven Habits of Highly Effective People*, we are expressing our telos. Personal and corporate vision statements, goals lists, even New Year's resolutions, all express our telos, the direction that we are heading.

The notion of telos also conveys the principles or values by which we hope to be shaped in that journey. Our New Year's resolution may be "lose twenty pounds," but underneath is a value of living more healthily and living a longer and more productive life. Our corporate goal may be "start a youth-mentoring program," but that is shaped by a value of caring for our community, or perhaps of providing opportunities to kids that we were given. Telos is always a goal, but it cannot be separated from the value that shapes it.

From the perspective of the New Testament writers, our telos is not something we will have ever achieved. This is what Paul was expressing when he said, "Not that I have already obtained this or am already perfect; but I press on to make it my own, because Christ Jesus has made me his own" (Phil. 3:12 ESV). In scripture, the telos is a statement of that place to which we are heading.

By contrast, much of our contemporary theological questions have to do with ontology. (Forgive the technical lingo here—we'll get through this soon.) Ontology is a branch of philosophy that is more concerned with existence, where things came from, and what categories we can use to describe everything from personhood to thought to love to causality. The God of this branch of thought stands apart from the physical world; we talk about this God as *metaphysical*, as outside of the sphere of interests that human science can explain.

As the Enlightenment brought about an immense growth in knowledge, philosophers and scientists struggled to conceive of and talk about God in light of all that we now know. Inside the Western church, this conversation took on two distinct tones.[1] Within the more liberal wing of the church, we had the God who stands above reason. This is a God who was to be experienced, but could never be known, because God does not fit within a convenient scientific schema. Thus, for many American Christians, God is somewhere, out there, but only to be experienced as a feeling.

Another wing of the church battled science and knowledge. These were the people most concerned about the loss of the ontotheological God, because the loss of this God would mess up all their categories. Darwin's publication of *The Origin of the Species*, for example, brought about a great challenge to categories of being. Liberal biblical scholars and German higher criticism brought about challenges to scholarship that brought about a great challenge to categories of knowing.

These differences have been worked out in our social formation. A popular book in my field of sociology (the sociology of religion) was by a man named Peter Berger, and it was called *The Social Construction of Reality*. In this book, Berger argued that we interact with others within social systems we create. Over time we develop conceptions of what the other believes to be true, what the other perceives as real, and that we then create institutions like churches, governments, and schools that reflect this understanding of reality.

But with regard to what we think about God, I have come to believe that there is also a kind of social construction of *theology*. Our concepts of who God is, how God interacts with the world, and what can even be known about God tend to shape everything from the churches we attend, the neighborhoods in which we buy our houses, the schools we send our kids to, and the organizations we form.

Thus, an hour from my house is an entire museum dedicated to convincing people that Adam and Eve walked on the earth at the same time as the dinosaurs. Their tagline is "Prepare to believe," embodying a belief that the primary goal is to get the facts right. This way of thinking has been described by Nancey Murphy as "cognitive" Christianity.[2]

The cognitive wing of the church has formed an entire industry and created multiple organizations dedicated solely to the development of apologetic arguments for the Christian faith. When they quote John 14:6, they emphasize the statement that Jesus is the *truth*. Churches within this sphere of thought spend time in defense of their ideas about God, and Scripture takes on a sense of facticity that I often wonder if Scripture itself supports.

Experientialists,[3] by contrast, scoff at the cognitive Christians. They have long since decided that science is science, and faith is faith, and never the two shall meet. Thus, Jesus is *life*, but this is often a life without all the messy interruptions, like Christ's call to sell everything and follow him in the *way*.

But what if both the experiential and cognitive visions are incomplete caricatures of our end game? What if we are being called to a broader telos?

DEFINING THE EUCHARIST

This is where I think the idea of the Eucharist is so helpful. Let's take some time to define that concept more precisely.

If you are like me, you did not grow up with the word *Eucharist*. In fact, I grew up without much of the vocabulary of the church or any sense of the tradition of the church. In my childhood years, I always thought the next big holiday after Easter was Mother's Day. And, in my youngest years, I might have told you that July 4 was a holiday celebrated by the global church.

Yet since the very beginning of the church, she has practiced one simple meal. In the account of the church right after Pentecost, the giving of God's Spirit to the church, Luke says that the Christians had all things in common, sold their possessions to give to anyone in need, continued to meet together, and "broke bread in their homes and ate together with glad and sincere hearts, praising God and enjoying the favor of all the people. And the Lord added to their number daily those who were being saved" (Acts 2:46–47).

The Eucharist, then, is a meal comprised of physical elements and given gratefully. I also think it can comprise a model for how we are to live. We see in Luke's account the three aspects of the Eucharist. First, there is the bread and the wine. The Communion celebration is, at the least, a remembrance of the physical incarnation of Christ and his completely physical act of redemption on the cross. Whether you believe that Christ is truly present in that meal is not of consequence to this discussion. Even if, for you, the Communion meal is nothing more than a time to call to mind Christ's sacrifice, that sacrifice is nonetheless a physical act that you recall.

Second, notice that the people ate "with glad and sincere hearts." This is the root of the word *Eucharist*, which springs from the idea of a gracious offering. The Eucharist meal, then, is a kind of happy meal (but thankfully without Ronald McDonald).

Third, the Eucharist is also a critical metaphor for understanding our role in society. I still get a little spooked when I approach questions about God through metaphor. As someone who was raised in that cognitive way of thinking, metaphors make me uncomfortable; they are not facts, or absolute and indisputable truths. And yet a metaphor is one of the most abiding doctrines of the Christian faith.

As the early church struggled to understand how Jesus could be both God and man, they conceived of a metaphor that we still use today, that is, the metaphor of the Trinity. This is not a direct biblical concept, although it seems quite supported by Scripture. It is not a fact, and yet it has become fundamental to the church's theological understanding, one of our ontological claims. How ironic.

A number of writers, including Colin Gunton and Stanley Grenz, have written about the idea of living a *socially Trinitarian* life. God the Father, God the Son, and God the Spirit all exist in tension; they are each one, and yet somehow they form a whole. This is the life to which we have been called, and yet it is not a life that we can verify in a lab.

Nor is it an understanding that comes from pointing directly to one scripture or from some desperate attempt to get back to an idea of what the church once was, as if returning to some pristine time in the life of the church is even possible. But as Luke Timothy Johnson has stated, "If Scripture is ever to be a living source for theology, those who practice theology must become less preoccupied with the world that produced Scripture and learn again how to live in the world Scripture produces."[4] What kind of world, what kind of Christian communities, does Scripture produce?

EUCHARISTIC COMMUNITIES

Thus, I want to present the idea of eucharistic community as an alternative telos to the models we have been given. And, I wish to offer this vision as an outworking of our theology, our very conceptions of God.

First, we have an understanding of Christ's body as composed of the stuff of the earth. As I discussed in chapter 3, we do not offer flour, yeast, and salt—we offer bread. We do not offer whole grapes, acids, and enzymes—we offer wine. The bread and wine are made of other elements but are no longer able to be described as simply a composite of those elements; they have become new creations. In the same way, we are called to give of ourselves to our communities and to the world. But, we are called as communities to do so. The individualism of today is conflated by Paul's description of the church as "one body in Christ."

The elements are also offered graciously. When planning for a Communion service, you do not think, *Man, I can't believe I have to give Communion to Mr. Smith*. At least I hope that is not your thought. Rather, something holy occurs during that time, and something about the gracious offering of the meal transforms a community, even if just for that moment. During that service, the whole of a room is bound together sacramentally.

This is why Paul was so harsh on those Christians in the early church who were gorging themselves at the eucharistic feast. In his first letter to the Corinthian church he takes them to task for approaching the Communion meal like it was the all-you-can-eat food bar at the Golden Corral: "When you come together, it is not the Lord's Supper you eat, for as you eat, each of you goes ahead without waiting for anybody else. One remains hungry, another gets drunk. Don't you have homes to eat and drink in?" (1 Cor. 11:20–22).

In the same way, we are to offer ourselves as "living sacrifices" in gratitude for what Christ has done for us. Our offering is to be given graciously and not for our own appetite. And yet this seems to fly in the face of another aspect of the Communion service, that it is sensual.

This is a word we tend to feel a bit uncomfortable with in our oversexed and overcaloried society. The word *sensual* is used so interchangeably for the word *sexual* that we think they are synonymous. But I want to use the word in the more traditional sense, which means to provide input, and even pleasure, through the senses.

We see the bread and the cup. We hear the invitation to the table proclaimed. We touch the elements, we taste the bread and the wine, we even unavoidably smell the aromas of the meal. The Eucharist involves our every sense.

The church, the recognized body of Christ on this earth, is called to be the Communion meal, as Paul states in Romans 12. Thus we are to be a people who engage with the whole of our being in the giving of our sacrifice.

In this way, the meal is physical. But it is also a sacramental act with an interpretive underpinning. In the Communion Supper, we are telling a story about the incarnated divinity. God drew near and continually calls us to, in turn, draw near. The Eucharist is an ongoing event of the church in which we can tell what that means and provide a metaphor for what that looks like.

In this way, the Eucharist provides an alternative telling of the other stories that have come to dominate the church in modernity. The church is not a community in some sort of eschatological waiting room. We are to be, alternatively, a group that is interpreting the story of a God who is already here and continually calls us to the thanksgiving table.

The Eucharist also provides an alternative telling to the story of

Buddy Jesus, the God of moral, therapeutic deism whose only call on our lives is for us to be healthy, wealthy, happy, shiny people. Rather, we are to a community of people who are, in the words of Henri Nouwen, to be "taken, blessed, broken and given."[5]

I also see the Eucharist providing an alternative telling to the militaristic God of nations and borders, the God who would consider one nation "his people," while another nation could be considered the other. But, in the Eucharist, we tell a story that there is no longer "Jew nor Greek, slave nor free, male nor female, for you are all one in Christ Jesus" (Gal. 3:28).

COMMUNITIES OF MORAL FORMATION

Our religious communities then have the opportunity to become communities of moral formation. Lisa and I participate in two communities here in Lexington, one of which is an intentional group called Communality.

We heard about this group when we were in England at a festival called Greenbelt. This is a really great festival where music and art mix with teaching on social justice and literature discussions. It happens every year in August and is well worth the trip if you can make it.

We were there in 2004, just as we were beginning to think more broadly about our understanding of God. We traveled from Maryland to England and there met a couple from Lexington, Kentucky, who told us about their little community. It was a group of Jesus-followers that were seeking to live incarnationally in the city and be, in very real and practical ways, the hands and feet of Jesus for those in need.

Several months later, at a gathering of people from Emergent Village, a group I have been a part of for a number of years, we met another couple, also from this community in Lexington. It seemed we could not travel anywhere without running into these folks, and they were not that big of a community.

Through a long series of events we ended up the following spring selling our house in Maryland and moving down to be part of this community. Lisa and I both had some fear about moving into the city, although in retrospect where we live is quite tame. We had never lived anywhere but in the suburbs, and we feared for the safety of our children.

Because our community often interfaces with those in need, those people in need tend to attend our Sunday gatherings. Often we get the homeless and those struggling with mental illness. During these times, we discuss Scripture, talk about our weeks, and encourage one another. Each gathering concludes with the Eucharist and then a potluck supper.

Shortly after we moved down we were at one such gathering. The bread was broken. The cup was poured. The elements were passed. In this particular gathering, I happened to be sitting across from my daughter, who was eight at the time. She broke off a hunk of bread. "This is the body of Christ, broken for you." She dipped the bread in the cup. "And his blood, shed for you." She took the bread in her mouth, and accepted the plate. She then turned to the man next to her, a homeless man dealing with paranoia. He broke off a hunk of bread. "This is the body of Christ, broken for you." He dipped the bread in the cup. "And his blood, shed for you." He took the bread in his mouth, and accepted the plate.

He then turned to the person next to him, and the sacrament continued. And I wept.

Our communities should tell a story of Christ in the Eucharist, a story that there is no longer Jew nor Greek, homeless nor homeowner, addicted nor clean, broken nor whole. Rather, we are all to be broken, blessed, and offered to a world in need.

We are in this way to be communities of moral formation. We have in this way also sadly offered a cheap alternative to moral formation in our churches. Morality has been reduced to not sleeping together before marriage, not taking drugs, and not stealing. But what if our communities started to form people who, in the words of Paul, "love from the center of who [we] are" (Rom. 12:9 MSG). What would it be like to be formed by communities consumed by God and God's vision for the world, and to present our community itself as an alternative vision to individuals consumed by the mindless consumption of stuff?

Body

Right about now you might be thinking, *All this discussion about eucharistic communities and giving of oneself to the other is great, but is our consumption really a problem?* Indeed, it is. On a very practical level, we are consuming ourselves to death. In the following four chapters I will walk us through some thoughts on the ways in which our consumption is affecting our bodies, the earth, our economy, and our communities. I conclude each chapter with some practical suggestions that can help as you seek to live into these ideas.

Let's begin with a discussion of the effects of consumption on our bodies.

LIFESTYLE DISEASES

According to the World Health Organization, more people die from heart attacks, strokes, and type 2 diabetes than are killed by war, famine, AIDS, tuberculosis, and malaria combined.[1] In Michael Pollan's great work, *The Omnivore's Dilemma*, he states, "The

United Nations reported that in 2000 the number of people suffering from overnutrition—a billion—had officially surpassed the number suffering from malnutrition—800 million." Increasingly, we are suffering from what have come to be called *lifestyle diseases.*

Lifestyle diseases are thought of as separate from communicable diseases, or so-called contagious diseases. We all understand how you get communicable ailments—you come into contact with a virus, a parasite, or some other funky organism. You can come into contact with these agents through water, air, and food, among other things. And, the medical profession, epidemiologists, and a whole host of other professionals have helped build antiviral drugs that can prevent the spread of communicable diseases.

But lifestyle diseases—what are they? Simply put, lifestyle diseases are those diseases caused by the way in which we live our lives. These diseases present more complex questions than the more binary questions posed by communicable diseases. Measles occurs whenever a child comes into contact with that virus, but lifestyles are not so simple.

Lifestyle diseases, by contrast, are a direct reflection on our consumption. As the size of our plates goes up, so do the rates of type 2 diabetes. Because we can directly link a disease like this to our appetites, this puts the effects of that disease squarely in the camp of our questions of consumption. With the exploration of lifestyle diseases, we can then begin to ask questions about everything we do. This includes the food we eat, the places we shop, the cars we drive, the churches we attend, the families we create, the television shows we watch, to name just a few questions that sociologists tend to ask when examining one's lifestyle.

But lifestyle is also an issue of privilege, a fact we are beginning to notice in the trends of emerging nations. After many years as a nation among the lowest per capita spending, "China is now the world's third largest buyer of luxury consumer goods, accounting for twelve percent of global demand."[2] Other Asian markets, India, and various Middle East economies are showing similar growth trends in the sale of luxury items.

Increasingly, nations we previously thought of as developing have actually matured into large consumers of goods. Some of this is just the natural ebb and flow of historic economic shifts. China, for example, had an economy twice the size of the United States in 1870.[3] But it is significant that as these nations develop they are challenging American per capita spending dominance in categories as diverse as fast food[4] to energy.[5]

So, perhaps lifestyle disease is communicable. You catch it through prosperity. In fact, as nations gain wealth, they increase in the risk of major health problems. Japan now ranks fifth in the world for heart attack risk.[6] Sixteen percent of Russian children and 7 percent of Chinese children are either overweight or obese.[7] (Don't worry, with over 25 percent of American children in the same category, we're still number one!)

But prosperity brings privilege, and privilege—the ability to make decisions based on our individual benefit—is itself a kind of contagion. In fact, it was this very contagion Jesus repeatedly spoke against. This is why he issued such seemingly paradoxical phrases as "the last will be first" (Matt. 20:16), and "If anyone would come after me, he must deny himself and take up his cross daily and follow me" (Luke 9:23). Jesus even kicks that up a notch later in Luke's gospel account when he says, "And anyone who does not carry his cross and follow me cannot be my disciple" (Luke 14:27).

America has the second highest rate of per capita income, falling only behind Switzerland.[8] What then have we, as a Christian nation, done with our privilege? I could quote more statistics, but let me tell you about what's happening in my neighborhood.

I live in Lexington, right between the rich and the poor. Ours is like a lot of smaller U.S. cities, in that the haves and have-nots live in much closer proximity than you might find in a city like New York or Chicago, although the effects of the disparities are often the same. In North Lexington—the *have-not* neighborhood—the food disparity is striking.

As part of some university-funded research, I participated in a survey of food access throughout that section of the city. The team found, as you might expect, that the economically disadvantaged have little access to quality, affordable food. In fact, there seems to be an inverse correlation—in other words, the poorer you are, the more likely you are to pay more for bad food. In convenience stores and gas-and-sips throughout North Lexington, I searched in vain for a fresh vegetable, or for any food item that had not been processed or chemically preserved. All I found were high prices for high-calorie, low-nutrition food.

It should come as no surprise, then, that areas like North Lexington help propel our nation to the top of lists like rates of heart attacks and type 2 diabetes. When we speak of the gospel in areas like this, what does it mean to talk about the Bread of Life when more than one generation has grown up with little more than Wonder Bread?

Further, what is the massive increase in these lifestyle diseases saying about the church, the corporate body of Christ? I find it increasingly insufficient to know that I am lowering my cholesterol and buying organic, when there is a pervasive problem in the body of our culture.

THE MIND-BODY CONNECTION

But our bodies are not disconnected from our minds. Not surprisingly, then, as our consumption has affected our bodies, it has affected our minds as well. American children have the overwhelmingly highest rate of attention deficit disorder, perhaps as high as 80 percent of the world's cases. Given all our choices, it would seem we have become easily distracted.

The United States also handily wins the competition for the country with the highest rates of depressive illness, with "9.6% of the population experiencing bipolar disorder, major depressive disorder or chronic minor depression over the course of a year."[9] As the song goes, money can't buy me love, and it appears it cannot buy our nation mental health either.

That is not to say we have not tried. This year American buyers of self-help tools—books, audiotapes, seminars, personal coaching—will spend an estimated eleven billion dollars. We spend more than one hundred billion a year on mental health services[10] and nearly double that on prescription drugs.[11] How's that working out?

We are not well physically and we are not well mentally. Our wealth, status, and privilege have not translated into a culture that is whole.

Our minds have not, perhaps cannot, escape this drive toward consumption in our nation. Earlier I mentioned that each one of us witnesses thirty thousand media messages a day, between billboards, television ads, and product packaging. But when I first heard this statistic in 1998, that figure was three thousand media messages a day. Times have changed.

Each year American industry invents new and innovative products and looks for new and innovative ways to sell us these products. But has this made us happier? In Daniel Gilbert's excellent 2006 book, *Stumbling On Happiness*, he defines the nuances of happiness as encompassing our emotional, circumstantial, and moral states. Are we moving toward happiness by any of these measures?

Emotionally, as we talked about earlier, we are a train wreck as a culture. Circumstantially, America is nine trillion dollars in debt, the mortgage meltdown is leading to unprecedented foreclosures, all while we are locked in a war that feels unwinnable and seems to threaten our national status abroad.

Increasingly, our cultural morality is reflective of the broad marketplace of ideas available in our culture. There is still a view of morality, and a sense of right and wrong, that springs from our worldview, a point on which George Lakoff and Francis Schaeffer could agree. But increasingly even those organizations whose purpose is to help people engage in moral acts are realizing that they need a little help. American Apparel, a clothing manufacturer in Los Angeles that promotes workers' rights, uses provocative models in provocative poses to sell their shirts and pants. And a church in Tampa is offering to improve your sex life.

PORNOGRAPHICATION

Sexuality has become a powerful modern currency. The old maxim is that sex sells and, in our economy, it sells quite well. A banned 2005 Super Bowl ad for Go Daddy used sex to sell Internet domains and was one of the most talked about ads of that season. The Hooters girls have helped their employer sell a whole lot of chicken wings. Sexuality is tendered to market cologne, cars, beer and alcohol, vegetarianism, jeans, divorce attorneys, and magazines, to name just a few. And all of that is before you factor in the six to twelve billion dollars generated by pornography annually.[12]

Our minds and our bodies are increasingly subjected to the *pornographication* of our consumer products and our culture. Pornographication is a word I thought I made up and then discovered other people using it. I use it here simply to describe the way in which the growth in pornography, an imitation of true sexuality that promises gratification without all the messy work of intimacy, is a signifier for a larger culture shift.

Pornography is defined as "printed or visual material containing the explicit description or display of sexual organs or activity, intended to stimulate erotic rather than aesthetic or emotional feelings." Like for a hamburger.

Do you remember the infamous Paris Hilton ad for Hardees? (or Carl's Jr. if you live on the West Coast)? This was an ad for their Spicy BBQ Six Dollar Burger. Naturally, it featured a near-naked woman washing a car while undulating seductively, which is about as clean a description of the ad as I can offer.

You would think that with all this sex everywhere around us, our sex lives would be off the hook. Are they? Well, that also depends on whom you ask, or more to the point, who is doing the asking. In a survey sponsored by the makers of Viagra, Americans are quite happy with their rates of sex. In the same year, a survey sponsored by the condom maker Durex reported that Americans are way below the global average of 103 times a year.[13]

Maybe the question should be: How would we even know anymore? In a culture where we are barraged with all manner of claims about products that will make us satisfied, by what standard would we even be able to judge our satisfaction?

For men, should we expect our partner to lather up before handing us a big juicy burger? Or, perhaps we expect she will be standing across the dance floor in a seductive miniskirt, just waiting for us to plunk our ice-cold beer onto the bar and send chills up her tanned leg. Even just the simple idea that someone else exists to wait for us and our sexual pleasure resonates with something C. S. Lewis said about the seduction of pornography and lust, in that it beckons us to believe that "the harem is always accessible, always subservient, calls for no sacrifices or adjustments, and can be endowed with erotic and psychological attractions which no real woman can rival."[14]

Ready access to sex, one of the most primal acts in which a human can engage—this is a fantasy that we continue to be sold. And for our advertisers and marketers to connect that urge with shiny happy people who are wearing, drinking, eating, smoking, or otherwise consuming something they seem to enjoy, ties that into a broader story of ready access to which can be a deeply gratifying act.

Has this belief in the ready access to anything that might bring us pleasure made us happier, particularly in terms of moral happiness? Has it made us wiser? Aristotle had a concept that he called *phronesis*, which could be thought of as practical wisdom that can help navigate you toward your desired end, which he believed was our happiness (*eudaimonia*). Has our culture pornographication, the immediate gratification of our desires, brought us closer to happiness, that goal that Aristotle believe all humans would desire to achieve? And to think as followers of Jesus, has our cultural desire for quick returns, whether that is in our bedroom or our boardroom, brought us closer to our goal of being found in a eucharistic community of people seeking to follow in the way of Jesus?

SOME SUGGESTIONS

What are we to do about this consumption? How can we as Christians, as people meant to live into the eucharistic model of Christ, find an alternative to the models of consumption offered to us? In this section, and in each of the next three chapters as well, I am going to offer some suggestions that I have found to be quite helpful. These are not "Five Easy Steps to Lower Your Consumption." Others have offered those lists, and if you find them helpful, then please, by all means, give them a try.

Rather, I would like to offer some suggested practices that have been an important part of my journey toward being more aware of my consumption, toward finding myself in a community of people seeking the same goal, and toward living more and more into the model of Christ.

Suggestion:
Plant a Garden

If you want to understand that there is no ready access in this world, put a plant in the ground. And if you really want to learn this lesson, start with a seed. It does not really matter what you plant, although food is a good thing to try. Wendell Berry once said, "We learn from our gardens to deal with the most urgent question of the time: How much is enough?"

A few years ago I was asked to address a group of mostly mainline pastors to speak about how they could engage their congregation in issues of global hunger. I told them to grow a garden. They looked disappointed. The simple fact is that I have absolutely no idea how to solve world hunger, nor am I altogether sure it is a problem for me to solve. But for the last several years I have tried to grow my own food in the city of Lexington. It's pretty hard. What I have gained is the knowledge of the difficulties in solving hunger issues, as well as some sense of gratitude for the food I do have, as well as a sense of the beauty of waiting.

I also think of planting a garden as a simple step in the revolution to transform life from the erotic to the aesthetic. There is nothing sexual about my tomatoes. But there is something good in them; they are reminders of the organic nature of this world. When cared for, they stand as a monument to the beauty of creation, with red and green and yellow, they burst to tell a story of hope for the future.

And, when tended, my plants connect me with the wisdom that can only be gained from a goal worth pursuing, as well as to connect me with fruit earned from time. An old Arab saying says "Old men plant trees." It is a reminder that we will leave behind something, and we have the opportunity to leave behind a world more filled with good and beauty, and more connected to the wisdom of the Creator.

Finally, growing food is a great place to start because I think it helps both our minds and our bodies. When you start to become known as that woman or man who is trying to grow some of his or her own food, it makes you a little self-conscious at the McDonalds drive-through window. And the engagement of the hands is good for the mind. Little in my life has brought me as much mental relaxation as digging my hands in the dirt.

Suggestion:
Develop Prayers of Gratitude

One easy practice to incorporate into your daily life is simple prayers of gratitude. At dinner, take time to thank God for all of the hands that got the food to your table. The food you eat did not start at the grocery store. It was grown or raised on a farm, harvested or slaughtered, packaged and possibly frozen, boxed up, put on a truck, driven, taken off a truck, put in stock, and bought by you via the checkout person, assuming your grocery store does not have self-check.

Taking time to offer prayers of gratitude and to pray for blessing for each of those people in the process reminds you that food does not come to you in some ready-access schema. Even if you buy "fast" food, it is a long time in getting to you.

The same kinds of prayers can be offered for the clothes you are standing in the checkout line about to purchase. A whole group of unseen hands sewed, boxed, trucked, and displayed those pants or that shirt.

Suggestion:
Eat Together

One great casualty of our instant gratification culture is the idea of eating together. This is an easy one to change. Eat together with your family. Eat together as a church or faith community. Eat together with your neighbors.

There is an entire movement toward this end, called the *slow food movement*.[15] These are people dedicated to the aesthetic and emotional elements of a meal. They are committed to the true sensuality of food—the tastes surely, but also the smells and the sights and the feels and the sounds. Something happens when we eat together. Maybe this is why Jesus held out such hope for a meal.

8
Earth

We are going to turn now to discussions of the effect of our consumption of the earth. In the past century humanity has consumed more than half of the world's nonrenewable resources. How long can this last? And what are some of the effects of this consumption?

Environmentalism is certainly a hot topic these days. Issues like global climate change have taken a front seat in our current political theater, seemingly out of nowhere. In the *New York Times*, from 1981 through 2004, there were seven articles that dealt with the intersection of evangelical Christianity and the environment. From 2005 through 2007, the *New York Times* had twenty-nine articles about the same subject.[1] Something is starting to happen.

In a special that aired on public television titled "Is God Green?" Bill Moyers examined this phenomenon. A small number of Christian organizations have sprung up without much attention from the church or the media in the past several decades to awaken followers of Jesus to the need to care for the environment, including the Au Sable Institute, the Evangelical Environmental Network, Restoring Eden, the Creation Care Studies Program, A Rocha, and Christians for the Mountains.

A number of evangelical writers have published substantial thoughts on the call for Christians to care about the environment. Most notable among these is perhaps Dr. Matthew Sleeth's book, *Serve God, Save the Planet*. But this conversation is taking place in local churches as well, and not just at the broad, national level. The pastor of one suburban megachurch in the Lexington area recently committed to riding his bike for a full year as a way to make his congregation more aware of our nation's use of gas.

Evangelicals' engagement with the environment has caused more than its fair share of political upheaval. In fact, of the twenty-nine articles from *The New York Times* mentioned earlier, nine of them dealt with the political threat of evangelical environmentalism to conservatism, the Republican Party, or both. Richard Cizik, the recently converted environmentalist and political head of the National Association of Evangelicals, was publicly chastised by Focus on the Family founder James Dobson; American Family Association chairman Don Wildmon; and Family Research Council president Tony Perkins.[2] They feared his discussion of global climate change would "shift the emphasis away from the great moral issues of our time,"[3] those issues being, in their estimation, homosexuality and abortion.

These are great moral issues. Abortion is always a tragedy and always an admission of the failure of society. The logic behind abortion is, I believe, rooted in a belief that we discussed earlier, that place called *away*. While the church and, much to their credit, conservative, prolife Christians, have been at the forefront of the crisis pregnancy movement, there are still many social divides to be crossed if we seek to eliminate abortion.

Homosexuality is, likewise, a great moral issue of our time, despite being limited in the public discussion to political struggles and silly questions over things like constitutional amendments.

But care for the environment is deeply rooted in a Judeo-Christian worldview. It was one of the first commands given to humans in the biblical story. Thus, it is also one of the great moral issues of our time. It also should be a slam-dunk for American Christians to find important and to consider doing something about, and survey data seems to bear this out. In a poll conducted for the Evangelical Climate Initiative,[4] among evangelical Christians:

- 84 percent support legislation to reduce carbon emissions, and 70 percent would support that legislation even if it costs $15 a month per household.
- 54 percent are more likely to support a candidate who supports legislation to curb global warming; only 10 percent are less likely support a candidate who seeks to curb it.

FOOD

So I feel like I am on safe footing here, especially when you consider the fact that Christians around the globe display similar statistics regarding care for the creation. But where best to start? It would be all too easy to get lost in the issue of global climate change, an issue that has received a great deal of press attention, and to spend too much time pouring through arcane data about melting polar ice caps and rising sea tides. Perhaps we could start with an issue related to global consumption that has only recently come into the broader environmental conversation but may be a much easier place to start: the issue of food.

We have already talked about lifestyle diseases, but permit me to spend a few more moments to tie that argument into the issue of the consumption of the earth. Rates of hearts attacks and strokes are on the rise. According to the Centers for Disease Control, the "prevalence of diabetes rose 5 percent annually since 1990."[5] But are there other factors than simply our gross national appetite that are contributing to the growth of these ailments?

There certainly are. And one of the greatest of these is the economics of the food system. In Michael Pollan's research, he found that 250 calories worth of carrots costs the same as 1,200 calories of potato chips and cookies. A dollar will buy you 875 calories on the beverage aisle but only 170 calories of fruit juice. So, he concluded, "It makes good economic sense that people with limited money to spend would spend it on the cheapest calories they can find."[6]

We consume too many calories, in part, because the junk calories are cheaper to consume for those on a fixed budget. This is one factor that explains the disproportionate rates of lifestyle diseases among the economically disadvantaged. But it also connects our food system with a broader growth in food technologies that allows us to transform raw food products like corn into everything from Coke to the main ingredients in the Chicken McNugget.

The more we buy of those products, the more we feed a system of inequity that is harming those most in need. We must be careful not to become legalistic about this principle—I still enjoy an ice-cold Coke or a bag of chips now and then. But we also begin to understand that our purchase of high-calorie, low-nutrition foods keeps them in production for those who do not have the option or the inclination to shop at Whole Foods or their local farmers' market.

We must also begin to ask if this system is sustainable. Cheap corn is produced in rural areas through the use of large amounts of petroleum products. The corn is then shipped to manufacturers, again through the use of petroleum. Interestingly, one of the greatest common denominators in every aspect of our industrial food system is petroleum. This morning, crude oil reached nearly $140 a barrel, nearly doubling in price in 2008 alone. What effect might that have on our food system?

More than a few large private investors are betting that increases in the price of oil, combined with strong growing demand in emerging markets like Asia, will increase the price for all the food we eat. There is presently a strong drive toward investment in food production, with "bolder and longer-term bets that the world's need for food will greatly increase—by buying farmland, fertilizer, grain elevators and shipping equipment."[7] Wall Street is betting that the price you pay for food will go up.

And that is in a system that is already horribly inefficient. The average food item travels fifteen hundred miles to get to your grocery store. The USDA estimates that about 27 percent of food produced in America gets wasted or thrown away. The cost for this waste tops out at over one hundred billion dollars.

ENERGY

And speaking of inefficient, our energy is largely based on extracted resources, which are neither renewable nor cost-efficient over the long range. More than 50 percent of American electricity is provided by coal, which is increasingly extracted through a process of mining known as mountaintop removal coal mining (MTR).[8]

MTR is the method of coal extraction by which the entire tops of mountains are blasted away to expose quantities of coal that, proponents argue, cannot otherwise be mined by "cost-effective" means. This is a prevalent practice in central Appalachia, where perhaps as many as one-half million acres of mountains have thus far been affected in West Virginia, Kentucky, and Tennessee. Nearly twelve hundred miles of streams have been jeopardized (seven hundred miles buried) by pushing overlying soil and rock formations (termed by the industry to be overburden) off the sides of mountains and into "valley-fills" that cover the headwaters of Appalachian streams and rivers. Topsoil and timber loss are believed to contribute to flooding.

Additionally, coal extracted by MTR must be washed to remove impurities. The vast quantities of water used in this process are stored behind hundreds of earthen impoundments that dot the region. One such dam collapsed in Logan County, West Virginia, in 1971, killing more than one hundred people and destroying more than five thousand homes in ten mining communities along Buffalo Creek. Another impoundment leaked more recently into an underground mine in Martin County, Kentucky, in 2000, causing three hundred thousand gallons of contaminated "sludge" to flood the area and flow into local streams and the Ohio River. (The fact that newspapers referred to this spill as the worst environmental disaster in the history of the Southeast suggests the amnesia that takes place when disaster strikes Appalachia since, at the time nationally, Buffalo Creek was forgotten.)

This devastation of the earth is directly affected by our consumption. With over 50 percent of electricity in America coming from coal, the connection between you and the coalfield is as close as the light switch or the thermostat.

But coal is not the only problematic energy source. Our exploration for oil may be nearing the end of the time when we can extract this resource from the ground in an efficient manner. This phenomenon is known as the problem of *peak oil*. Peak oil is "the point in time when the maximum rate of global petroleum production is reached, after which the rate of production enters its terminal decline."[9]

If this economic and geologic understanding is correct, we have, in about the last one hundred years or so, extracted more than half of all the oil on the earth. To pump out the remaining oil will cost us more than can be reasonably retrieved from the sale and use of that oil.

JUST THE BEGINNING

Having said all that, food, coal, and oil may be the least of our problems. A crisis looms about water, with the World Health Organization predicting more than fifty million people will become environmental refugees within the next ten years, due largely to droughts and other water-related shortages. Think about it—a group of people one-third larger than the entire population of California will be displaced by water shortage. And, WHO predicts that this will increase over the next forty years, with an estimated 180 million environmental refugees by 2050.

We have planned insufficiently for the crises we will face. We have a food system predicated on cheap oil and cheap calories. We have an energy system that is tearing up our planet and may quite literally be running out of gas. And our inattention to global climate change is bringing shortages of water, one of the most basic resources of our planet.

SOME SUGGESTIONS

Suggestion:
Buy Right

As I go out and speak, I am regularly asked, How can I buy right for the earth? In what ways can I alter my shopping habits so that I lower my carbon footprint? Well, I am not a big fan of lists, but here is the order in which I try to buy:

First, buy local. The very first place I look when making a purchasing decision is for a local option. The creation and strengthening of local economies is one of the easiest steps toward lowering our use of petroleum. In regard to food, it also adds an important aspect of security—when I look across the table at a farmer I am buying my vegetables from, and he knows I will be back next week, there is a kind of trust built between us that a government inspection system can never rival.

One word of caution with placing this value first—it severely limits options. With clothes, you might not look as cool. With food, buying local tends to rule out the option of being a vegan, and perhaps even being a vegetarian, since it is difficult to build a healthy diet off local produce without animal fats and proteins.

Second, buy from sustainable producers. Sustainability is simply a way of thinking about our resources, or a way of creating products, that ensures that method of production can be continued indefinitely. It is producing today without diminishing the possibility of producing tomorrow.

Notice that I did not say to buy "USDA Organic Certified" or mention any other formal certification programs, from either governmental or nonprofit groups. I think those can be really helpful, and I am especially fond of the LEEDS (Leadership in Energy and Environmental Design) Certification developed by the U.S. Green Building Council for the building of everything from homes to malls to office space.

Use those programs where they are helpful, but in the end it is up to you as a consumer to learn about the sustainability practices of the companies or producers from which you buy. And as you seek out that information, visit company Web sites, ask questions, and send e-mails seeking data about sustainability practices, companies will increasingly see these practices as a critical selling point of their product.

If you buy local, it is almost always sustainable. There are certainly exceptions: Fifty percent of all the Pop Tarts produced in the United States are made in Pikeville, Kentucky, making them a "local" choice, but not necessarily a sustainable one. But, generally speaking, this is a good order to proceed in.

Third, buy from ethical producers. Some might be surprised to see this third on the list, but if you concentrate first on local and then on sustainable purchasing, you have almost always dealt with the issues of ethical production in what you buy. A big-box retailer may not buy ethically produced clothing, and a large chain grocery store may not have ethically produced meat, but then they rarely provide local goods and also rarely engage in sustainable production or shipping methods.

You will still have to pursue some ethical investigation for some products. They still have not found a way to grow coffee beans in Kentucky, so as long as I continue to enjoy the java I am going to continue to rely on Fair Trade certification for that purchase. But, with the other values heading the list, the number of products I need to be ethically concerned about is a lot less.

Fourth, buy aesthetically. My local farmer's market is awash with color and smells and sounds. I still buy clothes that look good on me, even when I am shopping at Goodwill. If our engagement with the creation is driven at least in part by our desire for beauty, it is okay for that beauty to be displayed in the food we buy and the clothes we wear.

And finally—this is not really a fifth principle, but rather an idea to balance all the others against—do what you can, but be okay with some compromise. Cost is often a big factor in discussions about how to buy right. Geography can be another. For example, in Hazard, Kentucky, a Wal-Mart sits on top of a slab of rock that is one of the few reclaimed mountaintop removal sites. Given the poverty of the area and the few choices for shopping within a reasonable driving distance, it would be cruel for me to condemn those who shop there, despite what I may believe about the practices of Wal-Mart.

But do what you can in buying locally, sustainably, ethically, and aesthetically. If you use this final principle to justify buying a one-hundred-inch-big-screen television from Wal-Mart because the store had the best price, you have completely misunderstood what I am saying.

Suggestion:
Think Wholly, Act Wholly

Nearly forty years ago an environmentalist coined the phrase "think globally, act locally." That made sense in the late 1960s, when only the wealthiest traveled around the globe. Thinking globally meant pondering exotic, faraway places.

This morning on the Internet I read the morning news from a South African paper and listened to the BBC. On Facebook I traded messages with friends from two different continents. I listened to music on my iPod with parts from perhaps as many as a dozen different countries. Tell me, what is local and what is global anymore?

We live in a world where distinctions like global and local are going away. So must our understanding of how to do life in the world. In place of these local and global distinctions, I want to suggest that we think wholly and act wholly. The biblical concept of holiness is equivalent to the idea of being whole, and so should our understanding of ways we can participate in God's work of creation, both in our local communities and in the global community.

Suggestion:
Get Out of Your Car

Maybe this is easier said than done. Maybe you are a soccer mom, or a hockey dad, or you commute to work an hour each way. I get it. But each step you take, or each cycle of the bike wheel in your neighborhood is going to be another way of acting into a new way of thinking.

As you start walking or biking around your neighborhood, you will certainly help the energy crisis, but that is not the real reason I suggest this practice. I have begun to see biking as a spiritual practice that transcends simple questions about the scarcity of resources. And, there are all kinds of things happening in your neighborhood—people in need, spots of beauty, surprises to be discovered—that you will not notice at sixty miles per hour.

In our global economy, the needs of your neighborhood are connected to the needs around the planet. Take time to see those needs. If you want to know how to connect your church back to the community, this is a great place to start.

9

Economy

I had a childhood highly typical of those who grew up in the American church—white, middle class, and suburban. My father was active in both our church and in an evangelistic organization named Word of Life Ministries. We lived in a gated community, owned a dog, and voted Republican. My identity as a child was quite largely tied to a sense of economic well-being.

As I look back on this there was an understanding of the way of Jesus tied to American capitalism within my Christian upbringing that not only went unchallenged in my faith community, but was encouraged in subtle ways. I am not suggesting that I grew up within the wealth-and-prosperity gospel, but rather that there was little clear differentiation between God's economy and Adam Smith's. Even the way we thought about missions was similar to the way American corporations think about business: We hired specialists.

Once a year these specialists from far-off places would come to the church and talk about their work in wild and exotic places. And we would pray and thank God that *they* were doing it.

If we were to think of the American missions movement of the nineteenth and twentieth centuries, we might think about how captive this movement was to the idea of specialization. As our American economy has developed, we have grown more and more into specialists who do one thing very well. But there was a time when people were more able to handle a whole variety of tasks, and that time was not that long ago. One hundred years ago more than 90 percent of Americans were involved in growing their own food; today that figure is less than 1 percent.

In the intervening time, we have become more and more connected with a kind of simplistic capitalism that disconnects us from our economy. In simplest terms, the definition of an economy is the aggregate of all our choices. Yet, as we have hired specialists for everything from the way we raise our kids to how to have fun, we no longer even understand our power to make choices, or our ability to shape the world in which we live. We no longer think of ourselves as participating in God's work of redeeming the creation, but rather see ourselves as being carried along within the broad stream of our choices. This has had a devastating effect on the church, on our understanding of missions, and on how we think about the economy.

The radical nature of the early church was due to many aspects, but one of the greatest was the notion that each person was responsible for living out the gospel himself or herself; each person was responsible for the creation of what two writers recently called "the tangible kingdom." But as the missionary movement developed, we created missionary agencies and a whole host of corporate structures for people who "do" missions.

Thus the idea of efficiency became connected to the capitalist model of kingdom production. We hired specialists. We externalized our costs. We took on capitalist principles of production in the way we thought about spreading the gospel.

And we have increasingly failed to be able as followers of Jesus to draw distinctions between God's economy and the mindless consumption of stuff, even when that consumption is destroying the very fabric of our financial systems. In retrospect, as I look back on my childhood, our economic activity at the time would seem positively frugal compared to the economic pursuits of the average American Christian today. Since the end of World War II, our nation has been on a spending spree, constantly upgrading our understanding of the basic needs in life, which now include cable television, one car per driver, and more square feet per person in each of our houses than would have been imaginable for all but royalty just a few decades ago. But this increase in the consumption of stuff has not been cheap.

Between 1980 and 2006, the ratio of household debt payments to disposable personal income has risen almost 23 percent, from 11 percent to 13.5 percent.[1] Keep in mind that figure was calculated before the collapse of the housing market, which is happening as I write this in 2008, so that figure is likely to increase significantly when the Federal Reserve recalculates it. In other words, as with other statistics I mentioned earlier, even when we make more, we spend more.

As a nation, it seems that we are waking up with the hangover of a long economic party. American national debt now stands at over thirty-one thousand dollars a person.[2] Consumer confidence is at historic lows. Bookstores are filled with books on the problems of excess and the need for simpler lives. Headlines predict impending doom. We are all looking for some kind of relief, like an Alka Seltzer for our economic ills. But a "plop, plop, fizz, fizz" doesn't seem to be on the horizon. Our massive levels of consumption have placed our economy in perilous straits.

GOD IS NOT A CAPITALIST

The church in America bears some of the blame for the coming economic crisis, if for no other reason than because of the candidates we have supported. In 1980, when American Protestants overwhelmingly supported Ronald Reagan, the national debt was $930 billion, which was about 26 percent of the Gross Domestic Product (GDP). The GDP is just a composite of all the economic activity of the United States, much like you might look at the bottom line on the income section of your tax return.

By 1990, halfway through the administration of George Bush Sr., the deficit was over three trillion dollars, or about 42 percent of the GDP. It now stands at over nine trillion dollars, or over 37 percent of GDP, after having been brought somewhat under control during the Clinton administration. That is not to say the Clinton administration did not help contribute to our problem of consumption and thus debt, but it did eliminate the practice of spending money the country did not have.

Please do not hear my words as partisan—I am not advocating for or against a particular party or candidate. What I am seeking to ask is this question: Of the candidates supported heavily by the church, particularly the evangelical church, how have they handled the economic resources with which they were entrusted? And what kinds of shifts in our understanding have occurred during these years?

The idea that we can spend without consequence, and that more spending always leads to a brighter future, has sadly gotten confused with the economic philosophy of capitalism. Capitalism is the economic theory fostered first by Adam Smith in his classic work, *The Wealth of Nations.* In it he offered a view of financial markets that were based on the private ownership of property, the lack of government involvement in trade, and the use of investment capital to increase one's financial base.

This has become the dominant view of the American church. In 1985, Frank Schaeffer, son of the late Francis Schaeffer, edited a book of essays titled *Is Capitalism Christian?* and sought to further the linkage of historic and biblical Christianity with that particular economic philosophy. A few years back, the leader of the National Association of Evangelicals was quoted describing one section of the American church this way: "They're pro-free markets, they're pro-private property. That's what evangelicals stand for."

There are a number of ironies associated with the belief that the church has been participating in a capitalist expansion of the last twenty-eight years, but perhaps the greatest is that our expansion has been driven much more by government spending than by free market forces. Take Wal-Mart, for example. That corporation did not use its own capital in a free market to build a transportation system. Rather, it relied on billions of dollars in government spending for the interstate highway system to provide access to small towns where its low prices, often made possible by government trade negotiators with nations like China, could allow it to achieve market dominance.

Or consider the growth of the Internet economy. The Internet, this global network of networks that allows for the exchange of ideas, and yes, dollars, was not the triumph of the free market. It was, instead, the triumph of scientists operating in Defense Department and government-funded university labs, creating protocols and means by which we could avert a national attack, as well as by which I can watch Carrot Top on YouTube. In other words, without government spending, companies such as Amazon or Google would not exist.

Much of our current economy is buoyed on the back of defense spending. When you combine the money we spend on national defense with the dollars we provide for foreign governments who then buy American-made weapons, military spending accounts for 43 percent of the federal budget.[3]

In other words, most of the growth of the past twenty-eight years has not been a triumph of capitalism, but rather a triumph of government spending. But here is the rub: This spending was combined with the most significant tax cuts in our nation's history. Thus, we had an expansion fueled by government spending while at the same time limiting the money we took in to run the government. This is yet another example of our belief in the magical kingdom called "Away," where all of our problems, including our debt, go—never to bother us again.

The interesting, or perhaps ironic, aspect of the church's sudden awakening to these problems is that all along we have had a significant set of resources at our disposal to help us answer the question of how we think about and use money, and how our nations and governments are to be run. But, as Walter Brueggemann once said, "The dominant scripting in our society is a script of technological therapeutic consumer militarism that socializes us all—liberal and conservative."[4] We simply do not pause long enough to question the script we have been given and ask if it resonates with Scripture, the model of Christ, and the historic teaching of the church.

That is not to say we really know those things well, of course. While a clear majority claim to believe in the power of the Bible to help them lead their daily lives, an even larger majority thinks the Bible contains the phrase "God helps those who help themselves."[5] Big problem. It seems that we have read into the Bible so many things that we wish it said, so many beliefs and ideas that would confirm how we have been living, rather than interrupting us and forcing us into a new way of thinking. Thus, because we see Scripture as authoritative and important for how we live, then, along with N. T. Wright, we should state, "We believe the Bible, so we had better understand all of the things in it to which our traditions … have made us blind."[6]

So what exactly does God think about the economy? The first myth I need to dispel is the notion that God is a capitalist. If you are currently a capitalist in your economic beliefs, you instantly began the process of asking, well then, what category describes God? Is God a Socialist? A Marxist?

But perhaps those are the wrong questions. Perhaps our attempts to classify God by our own categories are little more than an attempt to make God in our own image. Luke's gospel account contains one of the clearest teachings on this subject.

The religious leaders had been trying to catch Jesus in a rhetorical slipup, and threw a question about taxes out to the Messiah. Luke says that

> they watched him and sent spies who pretended to be honest, in order to trap him by what he said, so as to hand him over to the jurisdiction and authority of the governor. So they asked him, "Teacher, we know that you are right in what you say and teach, and you show deference to no one, but teach the way of God in accordance with truth. Is it lawful for us to pay taxes to the emperor, or not?" But he perceived their craftiness and said to them, "Show me a denarius. Whose head and whose title does it bear?" They said, "The emperor's." He said to them, "Then give to the emperor the things that are the emperor's, and to God the things that are God's. (Luke 20:20–25 NRSV)

Too often that passage has been interpreted to mean that there are some things that are God's and some things that belong to governments and world powers. Thus, if our government wishes to pursue policies that involve massive amounts of debt, impoverish our future, and provide far more dollars to blow people up than to heal them of disease and malnutrition, then that is just how the cookie crumbles.

But I tend to think Jesus had a bit more of a glint in his eye as he uttered those words. Perhaps one way we could reinterpret those words is like this: "Sure, the emperor can place his face on a coin. People can even print 'In God We Trust' on their money. But my economy is wholly different than a hunk of metal or a piece of paper could ever convey."

So I tend to think questions of whether God is a capitalist completely miss the point. But, let me be clear—even if Jesus were suggesting that two economies existed, Scripture is chock-full of teaching on issues like the problems of debt. Proverbs, a book of teachings that advances the theme of the foolishness of debt, states, "The rich rule over the poor, and the borrower is the slave of the lender."

Too many of us who were raised as "Bible-believing Christians" have often approached Scripture to affirm the things we wish to be against and to provide permission for things we wish to do, like spending frivolously without concern for the future. But we do not have that freedom. We have all too often interpreted the sexual teachings of Scripture as normative, while the teachings of Scripture, and particularly the words of Jesus, that deal with finances, care of creation, and radical community are simply viewed as suggestions or, even worse, as contextual. This has gotten us into a lot of trouble.

PAYING FOR THE PARTY

By ignoring some basic principles, we have amassed, in a very short amount of time, significant debt. State and local debt increased 55 percent between the years 2000 and 2005.[7] According to a report from the Southern Baptist's Ethics and Religious Liberty Commission, roughly 1.6 million American households seek bankruptcy protection each year.[8] The average American household, in a nation with the highest rate of Christians who see the Bible as normative for their lives, has credit card debts far exceeding ten thousand dollars.

Churches themselves have become laden with debt as we have sought to build bigger, better, grander facilities that can accomplish the mission of God more effectively and with greater flair. While exact statistics are hard to come by, the average church spends about 10 percent of its budget for servicing debt,[9] while investing somewhere between 3 and 8[10] percent on missions or any activities that leave the door of that church.

We have been sold a story that debt is a good, even the right, choice. Some of the people who sold this story were those most associated with conservative Christian politics. And so our economy has become a vicious Ponzi scheme, the kind of swindle that promises unbelievable returns without future liabilities for all involved. As I suggested earlier, some of our comfort with this may be based on the belief that Jesus is coming back tomorrow to enact a big cosmic do-over. Some of our comfort may come from the fact that we see such a vast gap between God's economy and the economy of the world. But most of it, I suspect, comes from a toxic mix of ignorance and our enjoyment of consumption.

Since most of us grew up without training in economics, we are not aware of basic financial principles that are at work in our present debt situation. The past twenty-eight years we have pursued an economic model known as supply-side economics, the financial principle that we if we cut taxes and increase consumer spending, all our financial problems will be solved. In the wake of that, we are trillions of dollars in debt as a nation, saddled with historically unprecedented levels of personal debt, and coming apart at the seams.

There is, sadly, no free lunch. Try as we might, we have not been able to make the law of consequences go away. And, because of these consequences, the American dream, as we have known it, is going away. Whereas in the past we might have held a pastoral task for shepherding Christians away from frivolous spending, in the future we will hold a pastoral task of shepherding people into a new era where our economy is no longer the superpower of the world.

SOME SUGGESTIONS

Suggestion:
Invest Differently

The first suggestion I would make to deal with the problem of debt is to begin to invest differently. And closely linked to that idea, we must begin to think differently about investment. One of the easiest ways to do so is to think of savings as investment. We must recapture the virtue of planning for the future, an idea that permeates Scripture, and is especially strong in the Wisdom books of the Hebrew Scripture, the Old Testament.

We also need to recalibrate what we invest in. We cannot, for example, expect corporate profits to rise each year, a fundamental principle in our stock market. Consider a company that sells paper. In order for their profits to rise you have to use more paper. Thus, if your paper company stock is doing well, giving you money to take an eco-tourism trip, those funds may have come from environmental damage driven by the use of more paper.

Suggestion:
Tithe Relationally

A few years back some friends and I started something called the Relational Tithe. It was a simple attempt to change the dynamics of giving. As I mentioned above, it seems to me that so much of our giving goes to hire missional "specialists," as if the call to care for the poor and the disenfranchised is something we can outsource.

In this project, we tithe into a common fund. Then as people are in relationship with others who have needs, they can bring those needs to the group. In this way all of our giving within the tithe fund is only to people we know, or are no more than one relationship away from. We support people in our neighborhoods, but have also had the privilege of giving to people in need on every continent.

I am not suggesting each of you join the Relational Tithe. I am suggesting instead that each of you begin to ask what it would mean to shift your giving from corporate structures into relationships of people in need. Right about now you might be asking, What do I do if I do not know anyone in need? Great question.

One of the reasons I like this suggestion so much is that it has the power to get us out of our pod and into the lives of people. So much of our consumerism is at least made possible by the fact that we do not know anyone truly in need. Beginning to give relationally forces us to change that dynamic.

Suggestion:
Spend Locally

Finally, spend locally. Much of our national debt is from overseas financing. Ironically, as a nation we borrow money from foreign countries to keep the cost of mortgages low. The increase in value of our homes made possible by low mortgage rates allows us to buy more things, often from the very countries that loaned us the money to begin with. The easiest antidote to this problem is to buy local.

Community

In this fourth and final of the practical chapters, I intend to ask questions about the effect of consumerism on our communities. This is a bit more problematic than some of the earlier questions we explored. I have tried to show you the effects of our overconsumption on our bodies, our planet, and our economy, and used various statistics to do so. But it seems that showing the effects of consumerism on community defies easy statistical explanations.

That is not to say that there are not statistics to make the case. I could quote data point after data point that demonstrate the relationships between consumption and the divorce rate, the rates of crime within families, and the percentage of children who come home to an empty house because of dual-income parents working for a level of income often way beyond Maslow's Hierarchy of Needs.

Similarly I could quote one of a number of studies that show little statistical difference between followers of Jesus and the rest of the world in terms of their level of consumption. Christians are just as likely to carry high loads of debt, buy bigger homes than they need, and load those homes up with all manner of useless stuff.

But I hope to take us beyond a high-level, numbers-oriented look at the data when we discuss our communities. I want to ask about the story we are telling when we consume as if there is no tomorrow. What is the message of the gospel if we don't think we have enough? And what is the meaning of the Eucharist, this joyful celebration of giving that is to be a model for all of us in our communities, when we are neither grateful nor sacrificial to even those in our communities?

I mentioned the missionary writer Lesslie Newbigin before. He had a big phrase for what we are talking about here. He said that our congregations serve as "hermeneutics of the gospel." (Hermeneutics is just a fancy word for interpretation.) In other words, the way we act tells a story; it interprets for the broader culture the story of Jesus. Our lives, and the lives of our congregations, become a kind of new gospel account, written in public and for all to see. If the American church in the age of consumer excess were to tell a story, what would that story be?

FRAGMENTED LIVES

The first section of that story would be a tale of fragmented lives. We all have this increasing sense that things are falling apart: We want what we do not have, and we have what we do not want.

Some of the products lived up to their billing. When I use my iPod, I do, in fact, feel pretty cool. Not nearly as cool as the pierced, black-shirted Mac store employee who sold it to me, but it definitely makes me feel hip. And, it causes me to want to buy a lot more songs. Do you have any idea how many songs I can fit on that thing?

Some of the consumer products fall short of their implied promises. An actress selling shampoo is selling more than clean hair. A buff, quarterback-sized dude selling razors is selling more than a close shave. Contained in these advertisements is some kind of implicit statement about the kind of people we are, or perhaps can become, when we use the right razor, shampoo, cell phone, clothing, and so on. These products, as well designed as they might be, can never make me Brad Pitt or Brett Favre.

But perhaps the least fulfilling product we have been sold is a story of God that is divorced from the life of Christ, Scripture, and the history of the church. Within the past two hundred years, the church began to pick up phrases like "ask Jesus into my heart," and "personal relationship with Jesus." These phrases contain nuggets of truth. Jesus joined incarnationally with the creation, and that act facilitated a kind of personal relationship with the Godhead that was not possible before the coming of Christ. Even the idea of asking Jesus to connect with our heart, desiring for our deepest impulses to be wholly connected with the God of creation, resonates with the story of Christ as told by those who walked with Christ and the church they formed.

But those phrases also give a false weight to the individual story of Christ and minimize the notion of conversion to Christ being a larger story of "those who [are] being saved" (Acts 2:47). George Barna and Frank Viola have a great discussion of these phrases in their book *Pagan Christianity*.[1] In particular, they discuss the way in which intellectual assent through the acceptance of certain phrases replaced the sacrament of baptism, an act that for the early church was the act of confirming one's entrance in the recognized communion of Jesus followers.

It was Dwight L. Moody who developed the sinner's prayer that was then made popular during the 1950s with the ministry of Billy Graham and with the development of the Four Spiritual Laws model by Campus Crusade. Charles Fuller developed the phrase "personal Savior" in the mid-twentieth century as a way to help sell Jesus into a marketplace of increasing consumer choices. Thus many of the most-used metaphors for understanding how we relate to God through Christ are quite new in the nearly two-thousand-year history of the church.

And I suspect that those soteriological marketing blurbs developed by Jesus marketers in the age of rampant commercialism sell a false understanding of the Way of Christ. Just like the actress selling shampoo or the chiseled model selling razors, the notion of a personal relationship with Jesus is not untrue, but fails to convey the broader reality of the situation. It sells "Jesus and me," to quote a popular gospel song, but fails to offer a warning label about the hard work involved in Jesus and *us*.

Evangelical, Protestant Christianity thrived in America in that type of marketing environment. Many people came to America to get away from oppressive religious systems and to make their fortunes in a wild and free marketplace built on a kind of Darwinian survival of the fittest. In that marketplace, it was tough to sell a religion that required commitment to the group. And so, evangelists during the Great Awakening and the period of twentieth-century revivalism did some product redesign and rebranded Christianity, the act of following Jesus, as something separated from all the mess of having to live together as followers of Jesus.

This worked for a while. For the bulk of our history, America has been of European descent, meaning there was both a common heritage and a common grammar based on historic Christianity. In that environment, it was easy to sell a religious message that resonated with some core of what people already believed but was free from all the mess of having to live out the standard, "love each another as I have loved you" (John 15:12), or the even more difficult standard, "But love your enemies, do good to them, and lend to them without expecting anything back" (Luke 6:35).

The marketplace of ideas and thoughts that made the story of individual salvation a good choice is changing. We now live in a global marketplace of ideas, where a multitude of religious options are now made possible with a quick search on Google. Whereas a person living in the nineteenth century may have had the choice of Christianity or the absence of religion, we now have thousands of choices of brands of Christianity, from structured choices like Roman Catholicism and Presbyterianism, to the unstructured options of Pentecostalism and Holiness churches, with seemingly every choice in between.

And with the data on church attendance and religious adherence, it increasingly seems indisputable that the individual story is not going to survive well in a pluralistic marketplace of religious options. A religion that costs little also becomes devalued.

I see this as directly connected to the fragmentation so many in our culture feel in their personal lives. We can try to fill our lives with cars and televisions and fancy clothes. We can even try to fill our lives with theological ideas, Christian books, and church leadership conferences. But these cannot fill the void we feel in our lives.

FRAGMENTED COMMUNITIES

I see a huge void in our lives as being linked to our need for, and lack of, Christian community. Interestingly, some of the greatest marketing phenomena of our day relate to the creation of community. Facebook and MySpace connect people across time and culture. Even eBay is a kind of community. Affiliation groups exist on the Web for everything from classic car collections to Persian cat lovers.

But with all deference to the geniuses behind some of those sites, I want to suggest that none of them can replace the notion of a physical and geographic community that shares a common understanding of God. For those of us seeking to follow the God of Abraham, Isaac, Jacob, and Jesus, we have a model in the Trinitarian metaphor that has existed for most of the church.

That model can be seen as demonstrated in the Eucharist, or in the Communion Supper. The meal is a commemoration of God's sufficiency. The Eucharist is a memorial to a life given gratefully on behalf of a world in need. And something spiritual happens, even if for you it is nothing more than the presence of God warming your heart.

The model of a eucharistic community is one of our best hopes of moving beyond the consumerism that pervades our lives, our society, and even our churches. It also provides a strong countermodel to the story of evolutionary human progress, a cultural narrative that has invaded the church. In my lifetime, I have lived through the small-group and cell-group movements, the seeker-sensitive movement, the friendship-evangelism movement, and am now connected with various streams of the emergent church, including the intentional and neomonastic community movements. But if we are not careful, we can fall prey to the same false belief in progress that has gotten us into the mess we are in, a story that confuses the narratives of newer, faster, better, and more effective with the story of the Rock of Ages.

Our Christian communities are fragmented and falling apart. Whatever the real statistics are on church attendance, the reality is that most of our churches no longer provide healthy and vibrant communities in which to follow Jesus with others on the same path. And if Jesus is just a personal option, one that can save me from eternal torment but has no impact on the way in which I live my life and the people I seek to share life with, should it come as any surprise that such a weak product is failing?

Within the evangelical Protestant church we have lost the DNA of Christian community. The American church has little concept of what it means to be "the *people* who are being saved." Thus, we must narrate a new "we." All of us who are seeking to be faithful to the Way of Jesus must be grafted back into a larger story of God's work in the world and to the two thousand years of history of the church.

This is not to say that we can become the early church, or somehow return to that, as if becoming something in the past is attainable. Rather, it seems to me that in order to move from mindless consumers of stuff to fully participating members of eucharistic communities, we must find the actions and language that can bring those communities together and allow them to interpret the power of Jesus to provide broad meaning for our lives here and now.

THE LOSS OF A MORAL CENTER

As a result of the fragmentation of both our individual and communal lives, we have lost much of our sense of true morality. In our public debates we often speak of what will make our national community moral. And yet the word itself, *morality*, is inherently a communal word. Individual morality is an interesting academic concept, but in practice it is reserved for hermits and desert island castaways. Morality refers to the sense of right and wrong as measured and valued within a society.

So, the place from which we speak of morality should be a community. The creation of a moral center is not an individual act, but requires a community from which we can speak. Because of this, we have a hermeneutical problem. We speak of the power of our values and our Christian beliefs to shape our nation into a moral community, yet we do not reflect that.

SOME SUGGESTIONS

Suggestion:
Act into a New Way of Thinking

I've mentioned this phrase before, *act into a new way of thinking*, but I want to highlight this practice here as a specific suggestion for moving from mindless individualistic consumers into fully participating members of a eucharistic community. I can provide data for you that will help you understand the problems of consumerism. I can offer biblical and pastoral words to encourage you to "present your bodies as a living sacrifice" (Rom. 12:1 ESV), to live a life shaped in the mode of the crucified One. But those words will fall to the ground without the integration of your hands and feet. What I would suggest, as you seek to inhabit a eucharistic life in community, is that you realize that the Way of Christ is actually a *way*. It involves action. And, through that action can come a whole new way of seeing the world.

Suggestion:
Pray the Daily Office

One practical way to act into a new way of thinking is by praying the Daily Office. If you don't know what that means (as an evangelical Protestant, I had no idea such a thing existed until a few years ago), this is a set of prayers, Scripture readings, and songs that a great many of the church are also praying on a daily basis. A great starting point for this is Phyllis Tickle's collection of seasonal prayers, *The Divine Hours*.

Why would I suggest something like this in a book about consumerism? Because I think a life in community is the antithesis of mindless consumerism, and a great way to start living as a follower of Jesus in community is to connect with others around the globe through daily prayer.

Suggestion:
Develop New Rhythms of Life

Lisa and I are blessed to be a part of a community that is asking what it means to be the people of God and to be followers of Jesus in a particular place and in a particular time. Among the ways our community seeks to answer that question is through the development of new rhythms that replace the rhythms of mindless consumption we are sold in our world. Here are some of those patterns of life that we are seeking to inhabit:

- Rhythms of food: We seek to grow food for ourselves and integrate more fully with the food we eat when we have not grown it. Getting to know more and more of the actual farmers who grow our food gets us out of the individualistic idea that food is just something we eat. The consumption of food is the most communal thing each of us does on a daily basis, and developing new rhythms around the meal is critical to helping us act into a new way of thinking. Lisa and I have even set an empty plate out at the dinner table, as a reminder that, just like the parable in Matthew 25, Jesus may show up at any time, in the form of someone passing through town, someone in need, or just a friend with whom we want to connect.

- Rhythms of service: We also, as a community, seek to develop rhythms around connecting with people right where we live and asking how we might serve them. For our community that takes at least two forms: We help resettle political refugees who come to our country from war-torn places like Iraq and Liberia. Also, as we grow food in our community, we bring some of it to people who are more than one generation away from eating fresh food, and help them develop skills like cooking and preserving food.

- Rhythms of hospitality and gratitude: Third, we seek to inhabit rhythms around the basic Christian virtues of hospitality and gratitude. It is far too easy to begin to see our homes as *ours*, and that allows the story of consumption without consequence to be told right where we live. But, when we renarrate the story we tell about the place we live that not only interprets for the culture a story of lives given gratefully on behalf of others, but it becomes a powerful teaching tool for our children to see that lived out in front of them.

11

The Practices of
Eucharistic Communities

How shall we then be eucharistic communities? I have tried to give you a sense of some of the problems with our consumption and of some suggestions that could help us imagine a place beyond the mindless use of stuff and toward grateful, sacrificial communities.

These questions of consumerism are not new for either the church or the people of God. So then, what are the practices of these communities I am advocating? What kinds of disciplines shape our communities toward this vision of the Eucharist?

I set the question up this way in part because the story of consumerism is an obligation-free story. Not only do we suppose that there are no future consequences for our actions, including the way in which we care for the resources of the earth, but we also tend to believe, whether we state this overtly or not, that the past has no claim on us. But, as Wendell Berry has stated, "The past is our definition. We may strive, with good reason, to escape it, or to escape what is bad in it, but we will escape it only by adding something better to it."

I also think it is important to remember that when Jesus said, "Go and make disciples" (Matt. 28:19–20), he meant, "Go train people to behave like me." In light of that, what are some of the practices that we see in the life of Christ and the history of the church that might help move us beyond mindless consumption?

PRACTICE GOD'S PRESENCE

The first discipline I would advocate is the practice of the presence of God. As I see it, this is, and was meant to be, at least as much of a communal action as an individual one. But, in our individual, "Jesus and me" way of understanding God's relationship with humanity, we have forgotten the very words of Christ, when he said, "For where two or three are gathered in my name, I am there among them" (Matt. 18:20 NRSV).

Seeing the work of God happening in community seems an appropriate antidote for consumerism on many levels, including the psychology of consumerism. So much of our desire to consume is driven by an inner dialogue, a story of inadequacy and longing that we tell our deepest selves. To counter that story, it seems to me that we must find ourselves in a broader story, namely the very presence of God that occurs within the gathered community of Jesus followers.

This is authentic Christianity, and it is at the heart of the gospel story. After the resurrection of Christ, some of his disciples were walking along the road to a place called Emmaus. Jesus came alongside and journeyed with them, although they did not identify that it was he. At the end of their time, he was revealed to them as the Christ, and then vanished from their sight.

This is one of those somewhat spooky passages that are often difficult to explain to those who have not already accepted the massive leaps of faith required to be a follower of Jesus. It is not exactly rational to believe in a God-man who died, was raised again, and ascended in his earthly body to once again be a part of the Godhead. But from the Emmaus passage, and from passages like the parable of the sheep and the goats in Matthew 25, we learn about the very real presence of Christ in our daily lives.

That reality sits in tension with the reality that, as Saint Teresa of Avila stated, "Christ has no body on earth now but yours." We are, as I subtitled my last work, to be "the hands and feet of Jesus wherever we live." Thus we see Christ incarnated in and through us, and in and through the lives of those with whom we interact on a daily basis, and those two seemingly incompatible realities exist together.

As we practice the presence of God, we also practice a new way of being in the world that can calm our fears and anxieties, emotions that often drive us to consume. Like the discipline in John 6, where Jesus took a few resources and turned them into enough for all, we can rest in the knowledge that, as our hearts are calibrated more and more to the rhythm of God's heartbeat, we move in tempo with a belief in God's presence and sufficiency in our lives.

PRACTICE THE BELIEF IN ENOUGH

The belief that there is enough to go around also ties into the presence of God in our lives. That is not to say this has not been a struggle for all Christians. Even the early church, which was living in the wake of the miracle of the resurrection, had to be reminded of the problems of consumption.

So the belief that there is enough is something we need to practice. We do not need to stuff ourselves. We do not need to act like the world will end tomorrow, and eat, drink, and be merry. We do not need to "store up for [ourselves] treasures on earth, where moth and rust destroy, and where thieves break in and steal" (Matt. 6:19).

I confess that I am not good at this practice. As the youngest of six children, some of my earliest memories are of feeling there would not be enough. And I am fed the message of insufficiency on a daily basis, from the car I do not have, to the sex life I should be striving toward. Thus to begin to truly believe there is enough is a radical countercultural statement, and a practice I must inhabit.

Just like practicing the presence of God in our lives, practicing the belief that there is enough is something much more easily done in community. As Lisa and I have sought to move toward a belief in the sufficiency of the Creator and the creation, we have been aided by other community members seeking to practice the same belief, and to inspire others to do the same.

PRACTICE GRATITUDE

We must also learn to practice gratitude. We often consider gratitude something one possesses, but I see it as a discipline we must inhabit, and as both a verb and an adjective we must strive for. Like the concept *community*, gratitude is much harder to grasp in action and in description. We can say we have community because we live near others, or we know our neighbors, or we go to church with other followers of Jesus. But to inhabit the values of community, to be shaped into a new narrative of "we" that competes against the dominant cultural story of "me," that takes practice.

In the same way it will take practice for the value of gratitude, and the regular demonstration of gratitude, to permeate our lives. It is not something we can simply possess and be done with.

As we practice the verb of being grateful, and as the adjective of gratitude comes to shape us more and more, we will find the issues of consumption being less front and center. And, I truly believe that much of our culture's understanding of sin and foolishness can be shaped by a more truly Christ-centered understanding of what it means to live as a child of God.

This practice can help replace some of the insufficient standards of morality that look mostly at binary issues of sexuality and not at the broader sense of the kind of life to which God is calling us. Consider this verse from Ezekiel 16: "This was the guilt of your sister Sodom: she and her daughters had pride, excess of food, and prosperous ease, but did not aid the poor and needy" (Ezek. 16:49 ESV). Did you catch that? The prophet is calling out the sin of Sodom and naming it as "excess of food and prosperous ease." Does that sounds familiar?

The practice of gratitude is a must-have for eucharistic communities. And, it is a sign of healthy communities. In some recent research, Christine Pohl, author of the important book on hospitality, *Making Room*, describes the four characteristics of healthy Christian communities as gratitude, hospitality, promise keeping, and truth telling. Imagine communities shaped by these standards. Imagine the changes in us, in our communities, and our families, if gratitude became deeply ingrained in all we do.

PRACTICE CELEBRATION

This may best be understood as a corollary of the last practice, gratitude. But an important component of the practice of gratitude is remembering to celebrate what we do have. Eucharistic communities take time to consciously and openly celebrate the rich sets of friendships and networks that are formed when one lives in gratitude. They take the time to celebrate passages, such as reaching adulthood, marriage, and college graduation. If these are beginning to sound just like rituals, then you are starting to catch on to what I mean by the word *practice*.

PRACTICE GIVING

Finally, eucharistic communities practice giving. Or, perhaps, practice giving within community. As I talked about earlier, giving is often done as a way to dispatch our responsibilities. But giving as an act of community is more than just digging into one's pockets or sharing food. What would it mean to practice giving within our communities and as a statement of the eucharistic bond of gratitude?

I spoke in the last chapter of the concept of tithing relationally or transforming all of our giving into relationally providing for the needs of people whose lives we connect with. As we practice giving and develop the networks that are made richer and more whole by our giving, we find new ways to truly embody the sufficiency that has been granted to so many of us.

12

To Be

As a Protestant, I was always scared of crucifixes. I was taught that fear from my earliest days. When I would ask about the images of Christ that hung in my Catholic friends' houses, I would typically hear something like "We don't celebrate Christ on the cross, we celebrate the risen Christ—our Jesus is not on the cross!"

And we do celebrate the risen Christ, the Christ who was brought down from the cross, was buried, rose again, and ascended into heaven. But as a Protestant I had no conception of the crucifixion other than as a transaction that made possible the redemption of my soul. The power of the resurrection gives us a hope for a future, one that can sustain us as we face dark times. In other words, the risen, off-the-cross Christ represents a hope in the future, in what will be.

Yet the power of the cross also represents a hope for what is, and for what we are to become. If Christ is remembered only off the cross, we miss an important step. My understanding of the cross was caught up in the finished product and not the process. I was taught to be afraid of the messy Jesus.

And is not the fear of mess something that drives our consumer culture? We buy new houses because they don't require work. We buy new cars because they run well.

But our telos, our end game as Jesus followers, is not caught up in buying something new, but in becoming something new. It is far more caught up in the process of what we are becoming than in anything we could become in this moment, or even in the transaction of intellectual agreement with the claims of Christ.

TO BE CONVERTED

And so I wish to offer some thoughts on what we are *to be*. The first "to be" I wish to challenge our thinking with is the need to be converted. We so often think of conversion as a one-shot deal, something that is accomplished and done. This fits well with our desire to achieve the finished product.

Perhaps it is healthier, and more resonant with the story of Jesus, if we think about conversion as an ongoing process, and one that seeks to impact every area of our thinking and our actions. Below are some thoughts about areas in which I would suggest we all need conversion:

First, we should be converted from a poverty of wealth to a poverty of resources. Beliefs about scarcity—whether it is the belief we will run out of a natural resource, or the belief we will lose an opportunity to advance our status—these fears of inadequacy drive the mindless consumption of stuff. Thus, for us to move into a more holistic view of our resources, we must, over time, convert our fears of enough into a comfort based in a belief on the sufficiency of supply.

Second, we must be converted from a view that finds itself fulfilled in the mindless consumption of stuff to a fulfillment found in the body of Christ. The view of ourselves within the body of Christ stands as a countercultural call to the mindless consumption propagated in every sector of our culture.

Finally, we must be converted from a paradigm of "earn" to a paradigm of "gift." That which we have earned is *ours*, we can do with it what we want. That which we have as a gift we hold loosely and are happy to share. Also, as we move from *earn* to *gift*, each of us can begin to imagine our lives given as a gift to each other.

TO BE WHOLE

Most of our consumer advertisements sell the promise that we can be complete if only we will buy their product. But is being complete the same as being *whole*? Moving toward wholeness, I am suggesting, is another step in our progression into a life of gratitude, found in community—a life that stands as an alternative to the false message of stuff.

What might this look like, this more whole life? To begin with, as I have hoped to suggest in this book, we must begin to find more connection between what we claim to believe and how we act. For too long, people have spoken of being followers of Jesus and lived lives that look nothing like Christ. And it is far too easy to succumb to the easy standards: Don't smoke, drink, chew, or go with the girls who do.

Instead, we are to live consistently with the message of Christ as told by the love of Christ: care for the least of these, dedication to a small community of fellow travelers, willingness to eat with the tax collectors and sinners.

And as it relates to the subject of consumption, we need to begin traveling more lightly. We have, I fear, too often traded in the call to "take up our cross and follow" Jesus for the call to use Jesus as a safety blanket and to then proceed as if we had not been "bought with a price," and that we are "not our own."

The call to live more whole lives also relates to the way in which we view creation. If the earth is the Lord's and we are the Lord's, then I imagine that our future as the people of God, and the future of the planet as the creation of God, are bound together.

TO BE CONSUMED

Finally, I suggest that we move from consumption to being consumed. How could we begin to recapture a sense of holiness that is based on being whole people and communities? Toward that end, I will close with the words of Paul in 1 Corinthians, when he said, "The cup of blessing that we bless, is it not a sharing in the blood of Christ? The bread that we break, is it not a sharing in the body of Christ? Because there is one bread, we who are many are one body, for we all partake of the one bread" (1 Cor. 10:16–17 NRSV)

A CLOSING PRAYER

May today there be peace within.

May you trust God that you are exactly where you are meant to be.

May you not forget the infinite possibilities that are born of faith.

May you use those gifts that you have received, and pass on the love that has been given to you.

May you be content knowing you are a child of God.

Let this presence settle into your bones, and allow your soul the freedom to sing, dance, praise and love. It is there for each and every one of you.

—St. Teresa of Avila

References and Notes

CHAPTER 1

1 Tara Parker-Pope, "The Voice of Attention Deficit Disorder" *New York Times*, May 22, 2008, http://well.blogs.nytimes.com/2008/05/22/the-voices-of-attention-deficit-disorder/.

2 E-mail conversation with Seth Godin.

3 This language is offered in homage to John D. Caputo's phrase, "Let us speak, then, of love," from his excellent work, *On Religion* (New York City: Routledge, 2001).

4 *100 Years of U.S. Consumer Spending: Data for the Nation, New York, and Boston,* "Chart 33: Economic and demographic indicators, United States, 2002–03" (U.S. Department of Labor, May 2006), 55.

5 *Statistical Abstract of the United States: 2007,* "Table 1217. Expenditures Per Consumer Unit for Entertainment and Reading: 1985 to 2004" (U.S. Census Bureau).

6 *Statistical Abstract of the United States: 2007,* "Table 1235. Sporting Goods Sales by Product Category: 1990 to 2005" (U.S. Census Bureau).

7 *The Credit Union Journal,* February 26, 2007, 24.

8 I want to balance this view of the importance of the story of the fall with Walter Brueggemann's view as expressed in his work, *Genesis: Interpretation : A Bible Commentary for Teaching and Preaching* (Louisville: Westminster John Knox Press, 1982).

9 Brian D. McLaren, *The Story We Find Ourselves In: Further Adventures of a New Kind of Christian* (San Francisco: Jossey-Bass, 2003).

10 Marsha Walton, "Web Reaches New Milestone: 100 Million Sites," CNN.com, http://www.cnn.com/2006/TECH/internet/11/01/100millionwebsites/index.html.

11 Rick Levine, *The Cluetrain Manifesto: The End of Business as Usual* (Cambridge, MA: Perseus Books, 2000), xviii.

CHAPTER 2

1 Christian Smith, "On 'Moralistic Therapeutic Diesm' as U.S. Teenagers' Actual Tacit, De Factor Religious Faith." www.ptsem.edu/iym/lectures/2005/Smith-Moralistic.pdf.

2 Ibid.

3 For more on this issue, check out Charles Marsh's excellent editorial in the *New York Times* on January 20, 2006, "Wayward Christian Soldiers," (http://www.nytimes.com/2006/01/20/opinion/20marsh.html), from which all the quotes in this paragraph were taken.

CHAPTER 4

1 Richard Kearney, Emergent Philosophical Conversation, 2007.

2 Robert Farrar Capon, *The Parables of the Kingdom* (Grand Rapids, MI: Zondervan, 1985).

3 A number of people claim to have first uttered the phrase "there is no away." I could not determine who said it first, but I know it wasn't me, so, if it was you, thanks!

4 Miguel Llanos, "Plastic Bottles Pile up as Mountains of Waste," MSNBC March 3, 2005, http://www.msnbc.msn.com/id/5279230/.

5 Alan Elsner, *Gates of Injustice : The Crisis in America's Prisons* (Upper Saddle River, NJ: Prentice Hall, 2004).

6 Fox Butterfield, "Prison Rates Among Blacks Reach a Peak, Report Finds," *New York Times*, April 7, 2003, http://query.nytimes.com/gst/fullpage.html?res=9D0 1E7DE1338F934A35757C0A9659C8B63.

7 Sister Joan Chittister, "Obedience and Action, Speaking of Faith," American Public Media, October 4, 2007.

8 "English Language," Wikipedia, http://en.wikipedia.org/wiki/English_language (accessed Dec. 1, 2008).

CHAPTER 5

1 Tim LaHaye as quoted by David Gates, "The Pop Prophets," *Newsweek*, May 24, 2004.

CHAPTER 6

1 For a more thorough discussion of these topics, I would recommend Nancey C. Murphey, *Beyond Liberalism and Fundamentalism: How Modern and Postmodern Philosophy Set the Theological Agenda* (Valley Forge, PA: Trinity Press International, 1996).

2 Ibid.

3 Ibid.

4 Gregory L. Jones and James Joseph Buckley, *Theology and Scriptural Imagination* (Oxford: Blackwell Publishers, 1998), 3.

5 Henri J. M. Nouwen, *Life of the Beloved Spiritual Living in a Secular World* (Cincinnati, OH: St. Anthony Messenger Press, 2002).

CHAPTER 7

1 "Noncommunicable Diseases Now Biggest Killers" World Health Organization, May 19, 2008, http://www.who.int/mediacentre/news/releases/2008/pr14/en/index.html.

2 Zijun Li, "Luxury Spending: China's Affluent Entering 'Enjoy Now' Phase of Consumption," Worldwatch Institute, Dec. 16, 2005, http://www.worldwatch.org/node/3864.

3 David J. Lynch, "Developing Nations Poised to Challenge USA as King of the Hill, *USA Today*, Feb. 8, 2007, http://www.usatoday.com/money/world/2007-02-07-emerging-markets-usat_x.htm.

4 Daniel Workman, "Top Fast Food Countries: American Companies and Consumers Lead World in Outside Casual Dining," Suite101.com, Aug. 29,

2007, http://internationaltrade.suite101.com/article.cfm/top_fast_food_countries.

5 http://news.moneycentral.msn.com/provider/providerarticle.aspx?feed=AP&date= 20080513&id=8623125.

6 http://mdn.mainichi.co.jp/news/20040925p2a00m0dm011001c.html.

7 Hope Cristol, "Trends in Global Obesity," *The Futurist*, May 1, 2002, http://www. allbusiness.com/professional-scientific/scientific-research/172919-1.html.

8 "Household Income in the United States," Wikipedia, http://en.wikipedia.org/ wiki/Household_income_in_the_United_States#International_comparison (accessed Dec. 1, 2008).

9 Allison Van Dusen, "How Depressed Is Your Country?" *Forbes*, Feb. 16, 2007, http://www.forbes.com/2007/02/15/depression-world-rate-forbeslife-cx_ avd_0216depressed.html.

10 "U.S. Spending for Mental Health and Substance Abuse Treatment, 1991–2001" *Health Affairs*, March 29, 2005, http://content.healthaffairs.org/cgi/content/ abstract/hlthaff.w5.133.

11 "Drug Spending Increases More than 2.5 Times in Eight Years," *Medical News Today*, May 18, 2007, http://www.medicalnewstoday.com/articles/71212.php.

12 There is a lot of variance in the estimated dollar figures generated by the pornography industry, but $6 to $12 billion is the most credible range I could find.

13 Laura Sessions Stepp, "How's Your Love Life?" *The Washington Post*, May 22, 2007 Tuesday, HEALTH; Pg. HE01, http://www.washingtonpost.com/wp-dyn/ content/article/2007/05/18/AR2007051801653_pf.html.

14 C. S. Lewis, "The Broken Image" in *The Complete C. S. Lewis* (New York: HarperOne, 2007).

15 http://www.slowfood.com/.

CHAPTER 8

1 Samson, SSS Paper, March 2008.

2 Adelle M. Banks, "Dobson, Others Seek Ouster of NAE Vice President,"

Christianity Today, March 2, 2007, http://www.christianitytoday.com/ct/2007/marchweb-only/109-53.0.html.

3 "Global Warming Gap Among Evangelicals Widens, CNN.com, March 14, 2007, http://www.cnn.com/2007/POLITICS/03/14/evangelical.rift/.

4 Evangelical Climate Initiative poll (Oct. 2007).

5 "Prevalence of Diabetes Rose 5% Annually Since 1990," American Diabetes Association, June 23, 2007, http://www.diabetes.org/diabetesnewsarticle.jsp?storyId=15351710&filename=20070623/ADA200706231182625856641EDIT.xml.

6 Michael Pollan, *The Omnivore's Dilemma: A Natural History of Four Meals* (New York: Penguin, 2006), 108.

7 Diana B. Henriques, "Food Is Gold, So Billions Invested in Farming," *New York Times*, June 5, 2008, http://www.nytimes.com/2008/06/05/business/05farm.html?pagewanted=1&_r=1&ref=business.

8 The description of mountaintop removal mining was taken from a paper I co-authored with Dr. Dwight Billings.

9 "Peak Oil," Wikipedia, http://en.wikipedia.org/wiki/Peak_oil (accessed Dec. 1, 2008).

CHAPTER 9

1 Kurt Richebacher, "US Consumer Spending: Consuming America," The Daily Reckoning, http://www.dailyreckoning.com/rpt/USConsumerSpending.html.

2 "United States Public Debt," Wikipedia, http://en.wikipedia.org/wiki/United_States_public_debt (accessed Dec. 1, 2008).

3 National Security and Veterans Affairs: Defense Outlays, U.S. Census Bureau, http://www.census.gov/compendia/statab/cats/national_security_veterans_affairs/defense_outlays.html.

4 "A Growing Creative Friendship," Emergent Village, http://www.emergentvillage.com/downloads/mp3/2004%20Theological%20Conversation/day1_part1.mp3.

5 "The Barna Update, July 12, 2000," The Barna Group, http://www.barna.org/FlexPage.aspx?Page=BarnaUpdate&BarnaUpdateID=66.

6 N. T. Wright, *The Challenge of Jesus: Rediscovering Who Jesus Was and Is* (Downers Grove, IL: InterVarsity Press, 1999), 17.

7 Chris Edwards, "State and Local Government Debt is Soaring," Cato Institute Tax and Budget Bulletin, July 2006, http://www.cato.org/pubs/tbb/tbb_0706-37.pdf.

8 Jerry Price, "Family Debt – Statistics," The Ethics and Religious Liberty Commission, Dec. 1, 2005, http://erlc.com/article/family-debt-statistics.

9 "Debt," Generous Giving, http://www.generousgiving.org/page.asp?sec=4&page=188.

10 Mobilization Division, U.S. Center for World Mission, Pasadena, CA.

CHAPTER 10

1 Frank Viola and George Barna, *Pagan Christianity?: Exploring the Roots of Our Church Practices* (Carol Stream, IL: BarnaBooks, 2007).

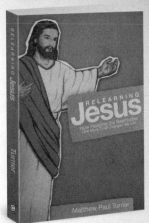

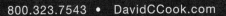

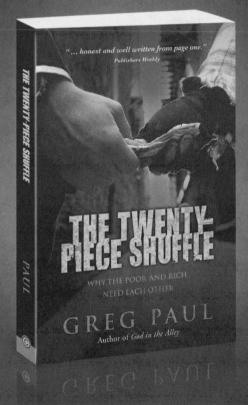